Sail With Me

The First Decade

By
Rebecca Burg

Boats, boats, boats. Boats are fun.

-Mack

- Small Talk Studios -
Edition: II

Disclaimer:
This book is for entertainment and is not intended to be a cruising guide. All cruising and navigational information, and live aboard boating information, are provided to motivate the reader to enhance his or her own knowledge base. Neither the author nor the publisher shall be held liable or responsible with respect to any damage or loss by misuse of the information contained herein.
Readers should be aware that cruising destinations and routes change and up-to-date navigational charts should always be consulted when navigating the areas and anchorages mentioned in this book.
Measurements are shown in American as the original articles were published for readers in the states. Apologies to my metric-standard using friends.

Some names and/or identifying details have been altered to protect the anonymity and privacy of some individuals in some instances.

Photos were taken by the author, or by Capt. Bill, except where noted.

CHAPTERS

Bahamian Journeys

1. Getting Underway
2. Destination Abaco: Little Bahama Bank
3. Leaving Mangrove Cay: A Lusty Battler?
4. Dinghy Mischief at Great Sale
5. Glowing in the Dark at Crab Cay
6. Dead Sailboats and Cave Creatures
7. Key West's Sister Village: Green Turtle Cay
8. World Famous Beach at Treasure Cay
9. Great Guana's Beachcombing Surprises
10. The Joke's on Bill
11. Squid Squadron at Nippers
12. Today's Forecast: Exploding Sailboat, Sudden Squall
13. Abaco's Crown Jewel: Marsh Harbour
14. The Man-O-War Time Warp
15. An Exotic Escape in Lubbers Quarters
16. Historic Hope Town
17. Wild Island Maze, With Wrecks
18. Real Life Castaways
19. Touring Eleuthera: Drunken Snail Surprise
20. Harrowing Rescues with a Side of Ticks
21. Crewing in a Bahamian Sloop Race
22. Crash Course Cruising Lesson

Southeast Florida Cruising

23. Crossing to Lake Worth, Florida
24. Coastal Atlantic: Lake Worth to Biscayne Bay
25. Cruiser Interrupted: The Do-It-Yourself Boat Yard

More Bahamas

26. Traveling with Sea Swan and the Dead

Southeast Florida, the Keys & Key West

27. Southeast Florida's ICW
28. When Squirrels Attack!
29. Key Largo to the Lower Keys
30. Key Weird
31. The Gifts of December
32. The Mysterious Marquesas
33. Loosing the Cruise: Hurricane Hideout Hustle

SECTION TWO

Becoming a Liveaboard Traveler, How and Why

Background and Preparation

34. Why Boats? A Brief Background
35. The mid 1990s: The End and Beginning
36. Single Female Seeking…
37. To The Florida Keys
38. Plan for Adventure, Now!

Living Aboard & Cruising Bonus Chapters

39. Crossing the Gulf Stream: Other Boater's Experiences
40. Eating Underway: Astronaut Food and Sprout Salad.
41. Fishing From a Slow Sailboat
42. Living Aboard a Small Boat: Money, Basic Needs, and Comforts

Two Strangers, Two Boats, One Crazy Idea...

You have a boat. I have a boat...we have an idea. Let's follow each other!

Escape into a remote, tropical paradise. Discover the beauty of the out islands with two small vessel sailors who live aboard and travel in each other's company.

An odd pair, Bill and Rebecca were from completely different backgrounds. When they first met, they had little in common, except for a love of boats and an interest in cruising. In order to live aboard and travel, they had traded secure, land based lives for an unpredictable and off the grid existence. Working to earn a living, they weren't wealthy, had no inheritances, or secret stashes of funds.

This book includes basic local cruising information about sailing to Florida's nearest exotic ports: Bimini, Grand Bahama, the northern Bahamian out islands, the Abacos, Eluethera, southeast Florida, the Florida Keys island chain, and nearby Marquesas.

Bill and Rebecca didn't need to go far and they weren't out to break records.

They just wanted to have fun.

Condensed versions of some of the following chapters have been published in *Southwinds Sailing Magazine*.

1

Getting Underway

Winter concluded and we'd been working long hours and saving to fund our travels. Captain Bill and I were still strangers to each other, yet we'd decided to sail in tandem to shores we had never seen. We were both singlehanded sailors who lived aboard our own vessels. Our mutual interests in boats and cruising to irresistible tropical locales had drawn us together.

A stoic combat veteran and fishing captain, Bill sailed an antique 36-foot Morgan Out Island ketch named *Defiant*. In a radical life change, I'd recently traded the bland security of the Rat Race for *Angel*, an antique 31-foot Bayfield Cutter built in 1978.

Inspiring each other, spurring ourselves into action, Bill and I studied nautical charts and made plans. Our goal was to sail to Bimini, then explore Abaco and Eleuthera before our seasonal work schedules called us back to home port. The time to truly experience life had finally begun. I was ready.

Embarking on a number of hectic shopping sprees, Bill and I provisioned in Key West. Fresh produce such as onions, cabbage, potatoes, and citrus fruits tended to last the longest onboard. Delicate perishables such as greens, tomatoes, and tofu went into a small icebox; this was before *Angel* and *Defiant* had been equipped with marine refrigeration. Bill stocked his icebox with steaks, milk, eggs, and butter. Our wildly different taste in food was a constant source of amusement and teasing. Bill mostly did the teasing.

The night before departing, we topped off fuel tanks and checked, then rechecked, our rigs and engines. Despite a sedate, subtropical night at anchor, I was unable to sleep. Nearby, nestled in *Defiant*, Bill tossed and turned as well.

Before sunrise, we restlessly stirred. *Angel* and *Defiant* left Key West harbor, the cloudless dawn a serene, violet haze. Eying each other's vessels, we raised sail and rode a southerly breeze along Hawk Channel on the Atlantic side of the Keys.

This was it. We were finally embarking on our first cruise of worthy distance to a new port. The route ahead was new to me and I couldn't help feeling some anxiety. Was Angel carrying enough supplies? Did I miss anything while checking and assuring *Angel's* seaworthiness? How long will the weather exhibit its present stability? Will I get my butt kicked in rough seas?

I scolded myself for worrying too much. Injuries or boat breakdowns could occur no matter where I was located; sitting on my rear, or working, or getting out there and experiencing a new adventure. Luckily, that anxiety would later fade as our journey progressed and I grew more confident.

Defiant and *Angel* dropped anchor for the night just outside of the city of Marathon in the middle Keys. After an uneventful night, we jumped back into Hawk Channel and sailed toward Key Largo. Our modus operandi was to drop anchor and rest overnight, then get underway by sunrise. For this trip, we didn't sight see along the Keys island chain since we were so eager to reach our first foreign port; Bimini.

A popular gateway to the Bahamas, the Bimini islands comprise a thin string of cays, rocks, and islets bejeweling the western edge of the Great Bahama Bank. The northern half of this string, North and South Bimini, is only about 45 nautical miles from Miami, Fl. The string's southern components are the Turtle Rocks, Gun Cay, and the Cat Cays. Travelers from southern Florida typically head to North Bimini to fuel up and island hop deeper into the Bahamas.

Staying within sight of each other, we showed Key Largo our sterns and entered the Gulf Stream. Admittedly, the day's crossing would be unexceptional, almost boring. Something I appreciated as a newbie to the Gulf Stream. Our sails rippled in a light 10 to 12 knots of southerly breeze. As the day progressed, Florida's coast disappeared behind us. We saw nothing but ocean. Vast and imposing.

I listened to the stereo, switching between an oldies station and NPR. After *Angel's* antenna could no longer capture the signal, I played CDs. When I turned the player off, a blanket of silence dropped over me. The sea bubbled and hissed along *Angel's* hull. The rigging softly clinked while *Angel* loped over the small waves, her bowsprit bobbing as if she was just as eager to experience a new adventure. It was sublime. This morning's subconscious attempt to surround my senses with noise reflected the social life I'd just left. Now, without aural distraction, I could contemplate.

Noise is an inevitable aspect of civilization, but it's overwhelming at times. Stores and restaurants pipe in background music, the ceaseless rumble of traffic reverberates through our cities, and the skies hum with planes. Our cell phones regularly startle us with insistent bleeping and the vacuous prattle of television shoves our thoughts into oblivion.

With such a din, there's little room for quiet introspection. If we do come across a moment of silence, many of us are uncomfortable with it and fill the perceived void with sound. A long sail on a mild day puts things into perspective. Moments of tranquility, space, and solitude, once we're comfortable with these things, heals the soul.

Without crew to keep watch, the length of time out of land's sight is mostly spent watching the compass and keeping track of the vessel's location. While in the cockpit and out, I wore a safety harness with a tether that could be attached to jack lines leading along both sides of *Angel's* deck. Hands are free to do random tasks thanks to a tiller pilot. It's like cruise control, but for sailboats.

Though the seas and weather couldn't have been more accommodating, I was still nervous. This was different than my home port in the Great Lakes, where coastal sailing was almost always in sight of shore. Though my old haunt was just as dangerous, I was in the middle of the Gulf Stream, a small part of a greater ocean. It wouldn't be convenient if something unexpected breaks or if *Angel* collided with an unseen object floating just under the water's surface.

Bill, admitting he harbored similar concerns, had slowed to match *Angel's* speed and remain in visual contact. He preferred that we arrived in Bimini together. We eased our anxious thoughts by talking to each other over the VHF radio; mostly joking, philosophizing, and commenting on our gradual progress.

"I wonder what's playing on TV tonight," Bill radioed at one point. "Not!" He laughed. "This is much better than TV. Hey, you know that a fast powerboat can cross this in about an hour."

"It'll take us all day," I said, realizing we'd have to be seriously wealthy to afford the fuel costs if we completed the same amount of travel in powerboats. "I know! Want to know what?"

"What?"

"I wonder what the rich people are doing right now."

"Hah-hah, watching TV?"

By mid afternoon, Bill spotted a thin column of dark smoke threading into the sky. Shortly thereafter, we saw the low, green profile of Bimini. Alice Town and Bailey Town on North Bimini is the center of the island's modest population. The single main road, Kings Highway, is lined with a few eateries, shops and bars. A diesel powered generating station sat near Bailey Town. That, along with the burning of refuse, created the smoky navigational aid we'd seen on our approach.

In fair conditions, boats can anchor in South Bimini's Nixons Harbour, which has sand patches at its southeastern edge that are 5-7 feet deep at mean low water. Nixons midsection is hard rock. Sheltered and more desirable anchoring is found near the channel's edge along North Bimini's eastern shore, north of Alice Town. Bill and I anchored here, where depths ranged from about 12 feet to shoal. The river-like current is strong and we each set two anchors, 180 degrees apart, on the soft patches of sea floor between the hard areas.

These small islands have a big background. In the 1920s, Bimini was involved in rum running during America's prohibition. Earlier, wreckers earned a living from the cargos of ships that ran aground on the reefs. Noticed just over 30 years ago is a half-mile long mystery consisting of symmetrical limestone slabs in 20 feet of water off North Bimini. Opinions vary on what this may be and there are disagreements on whether this is a man made or natural formation. To intrigue the tourist, travel blurbs hint it could be a road to the mythical "Lost City of Atlantis."

It was a relief to be out of the Gulf Stream and safely secured in our first Bahamian port. Tired, hungry, but eager to see the sights, we didn't know what to do first. No touring could be done until custom and immigration's necessary paperwork shuffle was completed. By then, it was late and we really needed to eat something and rest.

"What'll be your dinner? ANGEL hair pasta with ANGEL food cake for dessert?" Bill radioed, in good humor and joking about my boat's name as he usually does.

"We'll make pizza!" I responded. "Lots of it. I'll dinghy over in a few." Sailing all day has a way of instigating a powerful appetite, especially since I hadn't eaten much. Also, I sorely felt the need for a cool shower.

Stepping in *Angel's* RV-sized shower stall and pulling the splash curtain closed, I yelped at the stream of steamy water. The shower tank's solar heater hadn't been covered. I turned a valve and transferred some colder water into the shower tank.

Outboard not attached, I rowed *Angel's* rigid bottom inflatable, *Squishy,* the short distance to *Defiant* for our pizza date. Together, Bill and I planned our route over updated weather reports.

Our fair weather window was rapidly closing and we had one more exposed, deepwater crossing to do in order to reach Abaco. So, instead of spending the next day touring Bimini as we'd hoped, we would leave at sunrise and cross a deep slice of Atlantic Ocean, the Northwest Providence

Channel, while the weather was still cooperative. Two days later, we would be lucky we'd made this decision.

2

Destination, Abaco: Little Bahama Bank

Once again, chance had given us another uneventful travel day. It was early morning and the breeze had slowly dropped. So did *Angel's* speed. Her three sails sagged like wrinkled, forgotten laundry. The boom and its hardware, no longer supported by a full sail, clanked irritably whenever *Angel* rocked over a swell. Grumbling under my breath, I turned on the diesel.

The mechanic in me loved powered vessels, but I'd been spoiled by the unrivaled serenity of sail. I gazed at *Defiant's* pulling sails and made a face. Just ahead of me, the blue ketch was somehow able to maintain speed and enjoy full sails. I got on the radio and pressed Bill for his secret. After getting him to admit he was motor sailing, we passed the time with odd, random conversation.

"Submarines can hear your engine and know what kind of boat you are," Bill radioed.

"Submarines?" I responded, nearly dropping the microphone. The thought of a powerful military vessel lurking unseen below, along with nature's own strange deep sea denizens, was sobering. I stared at the cobalt blue water, rippling spears of sunlight penetrating the enigmatic expanse only so far. Olive green curls of Sargasso weed floated on the surface. After yesterday's easy Gulf Stream crossing, I wasn't as anxious today, but was still wary of the unpredictable.

The mild day wore on, *Defiant* and *Angel* crossing the Northwest Providence Channel. This Channel is a short, but deep segment of Atlantic Ocean that's best traversed in less than 20 knots of wind. In stronger weather, wind blown waves are roughened by the Channel's current flow and can present a long and uncomfortable ride. I didn't know it at the time, but the ocean current where we were crossing will often flow to the south, opposite of the Gulf Stream.

Soon, I was trying to keep my charts flat, which were stored by tightly rolling them up, and studying the access areas to the Little Bahama Bank. There are three places to access the western side of the Little Bahama Bank; Indian Rock passage, Memory Rock and White Sand Ridge. *Angel's* bouncy motion caused my parallel rules and dividers to slide from the chart. The stiff paper rolled into a loose curl over my face.

The closest marina is at West End on Grand Bahama Island. West End is Grand Bahama's oldest settlement and it's only 56 nautical miles from Florida's Lake Worth inlet. Boaters staying at the marina in West End should bring insect repellant and hatch screens to defend against the area's notorious dockside no-see-ums. They arrive in small clouds, nearly capable of carrying away small pets or children. There is no secure anchorage in West End's immediate, rocky bottomed vicinity.

Just a mile north of West End, the Indian Rock Passage is an access point to the Little Bahama Bank. Watch the depths and read the chart carefully. There are rocky hazards on both sides of this narrow passage. Once safely inside, the channel thins to about 8 feet at mean low water. After about five nautical miles, the channel opens up into the bank, where the depths range from 9 to 15 feet. The Little Bahama Bank is a surprisingly vast, shallow area of water. The seafloor here consists mostly of sand, silt, and grass.

Defiant and *Angel* nosed through the Indian Cay pass with daylight remaining. We saw Barracuda Shoal's tall, unlit stick marker, about 3 ½ nautical miles past Indian Cay. Instead of anchoring near Barracuda for the night, we continued over the Little Bahama Bank and toward Mangrove Cay. A firm wind had returned, allowing us to turn off the rumbling diesels and sail.

With caffeine and a careful watch, the occasional leap of over 100 nautical miles is reasonable for an island hopping solo sailor. Under a fading sky, we glided over clear waters and toward a tiny island that wouldn't be visible in the dark. The sun fell behind a smear of shifting pastel hues festooned with the neon yellow ribbons of contrails. Cool and humid, the brine scented breeze remained steady. The silence of twilight fell over us.

Still ahead, *Defiant's* navigation lights shone brightly in the darkness. Night sailing holds its own peculiar magic. One's senses seem to expand as the darkened sky unfolds into an eternity of stars. The crescent moon's platinum glow shimmered on the water and cast *Angel's* white deck and full sails in an otherworldly sheen.

Beguiled by my sailboat's subtle forms of seduction, I disengaged her autopilot. The interaction with one's vessel is part of the thrill of sailing. A slight push on the tiller, a tug on one of the sheets and we're gliding along in an exquisite ballet with the raw power of the wind and wave.

As she is always able to do, my four-and-half ton dance partner swept me off my feet. The rest of the world and its wearisome daily ruse receded. My old life of frenetic material pursuits was forgotten. In the groove, we sailed into the night.

3

Leaving Mangrove Cay: A Lusty Battler?

"**C**ome on *Angel*, get your freak on," I complained in the singlehander's occasional habit of talking out loud to the boat. Three sails limp, my unresponsive Bayfield drifted through a pocket of calm. At first, I wasn't sure how to interpret the scene ahead. A harmless looking puff of cloud had morphed into a rumbling, dark mass in a matter of hours. *Angel's* barometer dropped a few notches.

When three dark grey tornadoes, better known at sea as waterspouts, twisted out of the storm's ragged edge, I started *Angel's* diesel. Dashing on deck, I secured her sails and tangled my fingers in the sail ties. I was terrible at tying knots in stressful situations. The main was hastily shortened in a storm reef, ready to deploy if needed.

Saying something over the radio about not needing any more gray hairs, Captain Bill and *Defiant* were already motoring in the opposite direction. When a blinding shaft of lightning crackled ahead, *Defiant* whirled around, zigzagged like a cornered animal, and then dropped the hook to play dead. Bill shut down *Defiant's* engine and switched off her electrical systems. He was hoping to be less attractive to lightning.

We were in between Mangrove Cay and our next stop, Great Sale Cay. Out of land's sight, we were the only features around. Sailors are too familiar with that helplessly vulnerable feeling of having our masts, potential lightning rods, reaching into a volatile sky. There was little we could do.

The storm's gust front, briefly pushing forty knots according to wind instruments, rolled over *Defiant*. The ketch was buried in a dark curtain of rain. Earlier, we'd seen a large, odd-looking cruising boat that'd been traveling ahead of us. The vessel was just on the other side of the storm. In contact with them on the VHF radio, we'd learned the boat's name was *Arame*. They were also unhappily dodging waterspouts and rocking in the sudden winds.

Eyes riveted on the chaos ahead, I clawed at *Angel's* throttle knob; a sinister-looking silver skull. I'd installed it in a fit of superstition; my native side of the family believed it would scare away bad spirits. Today, it wasn't working very well. Diesel roaring, blunt stern squatting in a burst of power, *Angel's* bowsprit swung away from the encroaching storm. We weren't fast enough.

Angel careened sideways as the gust front overtook us. Visibility curtailed, I rounded up and dropped a single anchor. After traveling though plain air for several miles, lightning probably wouldn't notice whether our switches were on or not, but this rationale didn't prevent me and *Angel* from playing possum like *Defiant*. Thunder rolled around us.

A fusillade of heavy rain pounded on the clear panels of *Angel's* windshield-like dodger.

Rain jacket getting wet on the inside, I clung to the cockpit and tried not to touch anything metallic. *Angel* was bodily flung about by the jumbled waters and I was amazed the anchor wasn't yanked out of the seafloor. The storm was an impressive display of nature's potency. Its ability to quickly overwhelm a boater was frustrating. Madder than a hornet at my helplessness, I buzzed about in the cockpit, driven by an overwhelming desire to protect my ship. Nature overruled.

Still hot from being in the sun, the glass lens of an engine gauge shattered from the sudden temperature drop and dousing of cold rain. Sun weakened threads tore from one of the canvas dodger panels. When I heard and smelled my homemade brew explode its plastic container down below, I was disheartened.

Just completing its first stage fermentation, the unstable adult beverage couldn't withstand being shaken beyond *Angel's* normal, bouncy rhythm of sailing. A few gallons of hard work poured into the bilge. Dispirited, I hunched in the cockpit, blubbered incoherently and cursed the weather. It was *Angel's* turn to play protector.

It's understandable why so many mariners anthropomorphize the elements. Some refer to the sea as "savage" or "furious," and speak as if the weather is rousing itself specifically to challenge a boater who happens to be there. One worthy read, *The Secret of Mary Celeste, and Other Sea Fare*, offered a certain perspective that, at least to me, was interesting. The book's intro includes the words: "...to help preserve the image of the sailor of sail as a lusty battler against the ferocious assaults of wind and weather. His dominant ambition was not for gain, but to triumph over the sea."

Lusty battler? Ferocious assaults? Humankind's unfortunate preoccupation with war must be responsible for this antagonistic perspective. Triumph over the sea? Man is renowned for trying to control the natural world. Rivers are diverted, lakes drained, and mountains sculpted, but the ocean is one of the last bastions of wilderness that defies domination. Human haughtiness is useless here. Maybe this is why it is so compelling to sail into the sea's enigmatic embrace. The ocean has no place for false pretense and we must rely on our own ingenuity, wits, and each other, to survive.

Inclement weather is a fact of boating life, but with sensible planning, pleasant days outnumber the bad. We do indeed seem to "battle" rough seas, just by trying to get to where we're going. Also, storm stories have entertainment value. They're fun to share when we're back in safe harbor and if nobody's been seriously hurt. Inevitably, there's always some confused fool who'll have a dramatic, storm fighting tale for nearly every day at sea. This may be a ploy to seek admiration or display bravado, but what actually impresses experienced mariners is their lack of good judgment.

These people are amusing at the waterfront bar, but those new to cruising shouldn't be discouraged by such exaggerations. Experienced mariners work hard to minimize confrontations with poor weather. Paying attention to weather patterns, watching the sea and skies and practicing safe boat handling in deteriorating conditions helps assure more good days than bad. As was proven with this surprise storm, I'm still learning how to interpret the weather's mood swings.

The tornado ruffled blast soon abated, winds dropping and rain fading to a delicate mist. The warm sun briefly reappeared. I rubbed at a fresh bruise on my shin and inspected a scrape on one hand. Though I had some sewing to do, glass to clean up, and a new gauge to find, *Angel* and

Defiant were intact and eager to explore the next sheltered anchorage at Great Sale Cay.

When I started hoisting *Angel's* main sail, the cold rainwater that had pooled in the sail's folds poured over my head and into the companionway. Even this dumb luck didn't dissuade an agreeable sense of relief typically felt after surviving a dose of nature's rougher side. From then on, fluffy little summer clouds were taken more seriously.

While boating, I don't view myself as a "lusty battler," aggressively heading out to conquer nature. I'm out to enjoy and appreciate it. The sea is respected, even feared, but it's not viewed as an enemy. Still, it's wise not to underestimate nature's immense power and to be prepared for its unpredictable behavior. If there's anything to triumph over, it's one's own doubts and fears.

Now that is a worthy conquest.

4

Dinghy Mischief at Great Sale

Defiant and *Angel* continued to flee from the gray clouds and their quick squalls. Underway and reefed, miserable with upwind work, *Angel* peevishly jabbed her bowsprit at the lumpy seas. Sharp edged waves slapped and pounded the hull. *Defiant* looked equally as uncomfortable as she bounced ahead in bursts of cold spray. I was certain I could hear Bill's rigging clanking and rattling over the wind.

My feet and back were sore from the jerky, irregular bouncing. This was one of those times *Angel* behaved more like a bucking rodeo bull than a boat. Her 10-foot beam, or width, combined with a short waterline gave her an awkward, roly-poly footprint in rough seas.

My stomach began to protest, since what little food it held was uncomfortably sloshing about. I really needed an antacid, but was unwilling to go below and retrieve one. Leaving the tiller was not an option and it was too rough for the autopilot. If I left the helm, *Angel* would thrash sideways to the waves and saltwater would pour over the deck, into the cockpit, and in places that it didn't belong. To hell with putting my beloved in *that* position. I'd rather suffer a stomach ache for a few more miles.

Though I've never seen Capt. Bill get seasick, he'd once told me an amusing story from his deep sea fishing days. I recalled Bill's story where a Key West sportfishing vessel he was driving got caught beyond the reef in a bad storm. The ocean waves were so rough that debris in the fuel tank was dislodged. It immediately clogged the fuel filter. The diesel engine had to be turned off in order to change the filter down below. With the engine off, the sportfishing boat had no control and would violently roll from side to side in the waves.

Not only did Bill have to work around the fierce rolling, but he had to contend with eye watering diesel fumes and sickeningly hot engine room temperatures. Shortly after Bill went below to change the clogged filter, he popped his head out of the hatch and asked the first mate for two buckets. The mate wanted to know why the need for two. Bill responded that he needed one to catch the diesel in and one to puke in.

"Five miles to go," Bill radioed, voice hoarse with fatigue. It wasn't soon enough when two exhausted boaters slipped into the welcome shelter of Great Sale Cay. We saw a flawlessly shiny 65-foot sailboat without a mast, named *Arame,* at anchor in the cove. This was the cruiser we'd spoken with on the VHF radio earlier.

Perfectly new looking, there were no signs of a dismasting. It was as if the sailboat's crucial body part, the rig, hadn't been built yet. Curious about the unusual vessel and checking to assure she wasn't in distress, we greeted the couple on deck as we slowly passed by. All was well. The couple cheerfully responded by inviting us over for dinner after we were settled at anchor.

Bill and I were thrilled to meet and befriend Dr. Jim Harrison and Constance. We were curious about their custom built vessel, *Arame*. The couple explained how they'd built her, named in memory of a beloved black-furred poodle, from a bare hull. Over time, they'd customized her into a shiny, carefully engineered cruising machine. It took about seven years of hard work and they weren't finished yet. They looked forward to installing her rig, but didn't want to wait any longer to experience cruising. Just for the time being, *Arame* pretended to be a powerboat so an adventure could at least be enjoyed after such a long time working on her.

Jim's face was curiously familiar, and I soon learned that it was his friendly visage on the brochure in my toothpaste package. Jim, or Dr. Jim Harrison, was a holistic dentist for much of his life, had published a book, and helped create a line of natural dental products. A health nut hopeful, I have his toothpaste and mouthwash in *Angel's* medicine cabinet.

Despite having an abundance of room, *Defiant* and *Angel* anchored nearly on top of each other in this uninhabited island rest stop. My boat isn't large enough to warrant a windlass and *Angel's* anchor is pulled by hand. *Angel's* main hook, dropped from a roller on her bowsprit, is only a 27 pound Bulwagga with fifty feet of 3/8 inch chain that I'd spliced to thick nylon 3-strand rope.

A ten pound sentinel, simply a mushroom anchor, is used to alter the rode's catenary, a trick that allows the rope to pull from the anchor at a less extreme angle. This allows me to use a shorter scope, less rope, which is helpful if other boats are around. The sentinel also holds the anchor rode down and out of the way of *Angel's* keel and rudder should a current try to push her over it. I carried three more spare rodes, nylon rope, with chain and three other types of anchors; a fortress, Danforth, and plow. Likewise, *Defiant* carried a useful variety of ground tackle. What anchor we employed depended on the composition of the seafloor.

Defiant and *Angel's* intimate anchoring practice started a trend. Sailboats, always concerned about their drafts, often cue in on others to determine whether an area may be satisfactory or not. A small sloop wandered toward us, puzzled over our positions, then dropped anchor as close as she safely could. By the next day, we were in the midst of a concentrated flock of resting vessels. Since it was too inclement to travel onwards, we waited it out by spending more time with *Arame* and effecting minor repairs.

One task was to patch a pinhole air leak in the starboard bow of *Squishy*, *Angel's* inflatable. There was a break in the rain, and I had just the opportunity. I located my repair kit with rubber patch material, but the kit's contact cement had dried up. Searching *Angel's* stores, I found black 5200, a goo commonly used in the marine world. After the viscous, yet runny, adhesive was smeared on both patch and dinghy, the two were held in place with duct tape. The tape would hold until the gooey 5200 set, which would take all night.

Duties completed, I rode *Squishy* over to *Defiant* for a social evening. After tying up to the ketch's stern, I noticed a drip of 5200 oozing from *Squishy's* new patch, so I wiped the area with a paper towel. A gust of wind swept the crumpled towel out of my dinghy and across Bill's, which was tied nearby. I was unaware that as the soiled towel skipped along the floor of Bill's dinghy, it left sticky black deposits at each bounce. The towel blew into the water and floated away. I restarted *Squishy's* motor to retrieve the towel.

Meanwhile, Bill, loading his dinghy with gear, jumped aboard and stepped into a 5200 deposit. His big toe made black smears wherever he walked. Somehow, he got the adhesive on his fingers and was leaving a smeary trail of dark fingerprints.

"What the ●●●" I heard him grumbling as he studied his hands. "Hey, my white shirt!" Bill said, louder this time. Realizing what had happened, I slunk out of sight along *Defiant's* port side and tied up to her shiny, blue flank. I climbed aboard.

"Boy, I made some kind of mess," Bill said with a perplexed expression, vigorously wiping his hands with a rag. I slowly nodded, struggling to maintain an innocent façade.

Over a shared dinner, we studied our next stop in the pages of a cruising guide, and then watched a movie. During the first few years of our travels, Bill had a substantial VHS movie collection. He was slow in the costly process of swapping those clunky plastic boxes of tapes for DVDs.

That evening, I bid Bill and *Defiant* good night and returned to *Angel*. It was too dark to see the horrible mischief that *Squishy's* oozing patch had metered out to *Defiant*. By sunrise, the black goo had finally set.

"*ANGEL!*" I heard an exasperated cry. It was the first sound to carry through the placid morning. Coffee in hand, I bobbed out of the cabin. The grey weather had been replaced by bright sun and mild winds. Nearby, Bill was in his dinghy, muttering in displeasure and rubbing at a wavering, black smear on *Defiant's* side. *Squishy's* unconventional patch job had stopped the leak, but not without casualties. Now, I just had a little explaining, and a lot of cleaning, to do.

5

Glowing in the Dark at Crab Cay

As the sun rose, *Defiant* and *Angel* left Great Sale and tacked into an easterly 12 knot breeze. In sheltered waters, I towed *Angel's* dinghy. Though I'd pulled the outboard off, the tow still slowed me down as we headed, upwind, toward Allans-Pensacola Cay. After a few baffling hours of severely compressed tacks with little actual progress, we relented and turned on our diesels, motor sailing to make the short 35 nautical miles in a reasonable time.

Allans-Pensacola has a sheltered anchorage at its northwestern side. A fellow boater informed us that there was an abandoned U.S. missile tracking station on the island, but we didn't have time to explore ashore. Too weary, we remained on our boats and rested. For those who take the time to investigate this out of the way place, the sugar white sand beaches beckon.

The next morning was spent on boat chores. Using a needle and heavy, UV-resistant thread, I started some sewing repairs to *Angel's* dodger and bimini. Then, a bulb was changed on a navigation light. The wet-cell batteries were checked, distilled water added where needed. Interior surfaces, areas where black mildew had started to form, were cleaned with white vinegar. Using a 12-volt vacuum cleaner I'd found at a truck stop some years ago, I vacuumed *Angel's* cabin.

Organized and refreshed, Bill and I raised sail for an afternoon ride toward Crab Cay. It was a short trip, but, as usual, the wind was on the nose. Over the years of traveling though here, it always seemed that the prevailing winds followed the contours of the Abaco Sea. They'd be on the nose for the trip in and directly astern for the trip out.

Our destination, a low haze of green beyond the rippling seas, gradually took form. As our previous stops, Crab Cay was uninhabited.

"Hah!" I heard Bill announce over the radio as *Angel* pulled up near the already anchored *Defiant*. "I beat you by ten minutes!" Though the larger *Defiant* was faster, we still couldn't help occasionally racing and teasing the looser. As usual, it was Bill doing the teasing.

It was early evening when we finally settled in the semi-sheltered cove southwest of Crab Cay and Angelfish Point. The cove is a scenic spot at the northerly meeting point of Little Abaco and Great Abaco Island. The anchoring area is exposed to the northwest, but we weren't expecting any strong winds from that direction.

The water was calm, so I reattached the outboard to *Squishy*. Only in steady conditions was it possible for a short person like me to pick up the old 15-horse two-stroke and secure it to the dinghy's transom. Interestingly, the clunky thing was easier to attach than it was to remove. In rougher waters, a crane-like lifting tackle that connected to *Angel's* boom was employed as backup.

While I was setting up the outboard, another sailboat arrived and anchored farther out. Slightly larger than *Angel*, the boat's name was *Escape* and the couple onboard, Tom and Babette, hailed us on the radio to ask about the anchoring conditions where we were. *Defiant* told them our depth, assuring *Escape* it wasn't as shallow as it indicated on the charts. The cruiser settled closer. During parts of our island hopping, *Escape* would join us in a caravan of three.

Densely garnished with coconut palms, Crab Cay's pebbly sand and limestone beach resembled a postcard fantasy. Typical of the Bahamian out islands, a strong, floral scent perfumed the warm breeze. So in awe of the area's beauty, we just had to beat the sunset and investigate.

Dinghy beached, we wandered, stiff legged, up the sandy bank and into the palm tree forest. Immediately, we dashed back to *Squishy*, our hands flailing in the air. A dense cloud of mosquitoes pursed us. Exploring is best done at daytime and not in the evening when the bugs venture out.

That evening, I took the dinghy over to Defiant, Bill and I memorizing our next island destination with *Steve Dodge's Abaco cruising guide*. Bill's cockpit light was bright enough to read by so we explored Bill's magazine collection, both reaching for the newest issue of ▓▓▓▓ We foolishly tussled over it. My hand slipped and I tipped backwards, hat falling overboard. Bill reached for his boat hook and scooped it up. As he did so, the water around the wayward hat erupted with eerie, glittering green bioluminescence. Soggy headwear recovered and rinsed, we turned our attentions to the fascinating water.

"Here, watch this," Bill said, casting a lure and reeling it back. The water erupted in flares of fiery green wherever it was touched. The lure was a glowing oval that left a sparkling trail, and it had a larger luminous object chasing it. The larger object darted away.

"I can see the fish!" Like curious kids, we laughed and poked at the water with the tips of Bill's fishing rods, creating smoky swirls and sparkling splashes. It was a glittering submarine fairyland. This phenomenon inspired Bill to share a story about the time he and three Navy men were sitting in a lifeguard shack over the beach on the east coast at night.

While Bill and his enlisted friends were hanging out at the beach one night, a massive, luminous green blob with flippers rose from the ocean's depths and slowly started coming toward them. The four young and tough Navy men watched the glowing, fin waving mystery creep closer.

Hackles bristling, the fellows raced away from the supposed monster, not feeling very tough at the moment. The next day, Bill and his friends learned that a dead whale had washed up on the beach. It was right near the spot they'd been sitting the night before. The glowing green effects were the phosphorescent, microscopic creatures feeding on the whale's carcass as it drifted ashore late in the night.

Bill still kept in touch with at least one Navy buddy, Bill Knerr, a handsome, soft-spoken fellow who lived on the east coast. Captain Bill also showed me a photograph of the impressive ship that he and his Navy comrades served on, the frigate USS *McCandless*.

6

Dead Sailboats and Cave Creatures

With the prevailing southeasterly winds, heading south and transiting into the narrow north end of the Abaco Sea is a long series of short tacks. An opposing ocean current can make this leg of the trip a strenuous sail, especially for smaller vessels. Aside from the shoals, the Abaco Sea narrows down to about a 2 ½ nautical mile width all the way to Green Turtle Cay.

Angel and I lagged behind *Defiant*, the big ketch not as easily manhandled by the conditions. *Escape* had gotten underway earlier, Tom and Babette heading toward Green Turtle where we'd meet up with them a few days later.

Dodging the mile wide shoal at Spanish Cay's southern end, we tacked past this privately owned out island. Spanish Cay's resort, marina, and small airplane runway is open to visitors, but anchoring there is discouraged. *Arame*, her generator in need of repairs, took a slip there and received courteous attention. Just south of Spanish Cay lay our destination; Powell Cay, a mostly uninhabited small island.

Emboldened by a soft seafloor and our shoal draft keels, *Angel* and *Defiant* swerved and circled in a cove on Powell's western side. Our behavior was reminiscent of two unleashed canines excitedly inspecting a new backyard. The generous cove offered a comfortable depth of 8 to 10 feet, but we sniffed our way closer to the beach and anchored in thinner water. The seafloor is the typical out island blend of grass, sand, and crusty grit. If the weather's questionable, it's helpful to snorkel on the anchor to assure that it has gained good purchase. After we'd settled in and the silt cleared, a tinkling chorus of birdsong enveloped the serene cove.

A few other vessels were present on the bay's far side. A beauty named *Vineyard Passage* and another well kept sailboat had the name *Sea Urchin* on her curvy stern. We spotted just one small, unoccupied cottage on the wild shoreline. Here, we were sheltered from northerly to southeasterly winds.

Should the weather shift and blow from the west, boats move to the new lee near Great Abaco Island. The Bahamian settlement of Coopers Town on Great Abaco is two miles away from Powell Cay's anchorage. There's a public dock at Coopers and modest provisions can be found, but there's no marina or sheltered harbor.

The next day, Bill and I piled in the dinghy to explore Powell's unique natural and not so natural features. We nosed the dinghy around a miniature, rusted barge with a crane partially sunken in the cove's shallows. Weathered beyond utility, it looked like a good snorkeling attraction and fish habitat. Bill leaned toward the water, eyeing the swarms of small fish lingering in the wreck's shadows.

Leaving the barge, we idled along worn, vertical limestone bluffs outside the northwestern edges of the Cay.

Collapsed in places, the stone walls were eroded by the elements and pocked with large holes and small caves.

We approached a row of dark caves. I stood up and looked into one of the holes. A puffy, white face with glittering black eyes peered back. The face retreated into the hole. I cried out, teetering backwards.

'████████' I fell across Bill, rocking the dinghy and splashing us both. The dinghy's rubber rail scuffled against the stone cliff.

"What, what?" Bill said, helping me upright. "You okay?" He pushed the dinghy away from the wall.

"The holes–" I breathlessly pointed. "– spooky faces!"

Inquisitive, Bill carefully stood and looked into the caves.

"It's just a bird!" He said, chuckling. "You 'fraidy cat."

Long tailed Tropic birds were roosting in the holes. We respectfully backed away to give these wild creatures some space. I'd probably frightened these innocent locals more than they'd scared me. Around a corner, Bill spied another wreck. Out of morbid curiosity, we nosed around the ghastly sight. It was strewn across the sand along the water's edge.

"It looks like half of a sailboat," I said, pointing to what resembled a deck and cabin top with empty port holes. A rusted diesel engine, hoses, and an icebox sat nearby. We found the sailboat's bottom half a few feet away, just under the water's surface. It was a metal hull with a jagged gash in its side.

The forces capable of inflicting such damage were likely from Hurricane Floyd in 1999. With a surge and storm tide fifteen feet above normal, 150 mph winds, and torrential downpours, Floyd wasn't a storm that locals would forget. Grim faced, Bill prodded the wreck's edge with his toe. The sailboat's corporeal remains and violent demise would give the most stoic sailor the creeps.

Farther along the beach, a hand painted sign pointed to a path that took visitors up a scenic bluff. We'd left our shoes on our boats and were reluctant to follow the prickly, brushy nature trail. Barefoot, we walked the beach instead. Cruisers, who tend to be conscientious about keeping their valued boating destinations as pristine as possible, will find themselves collecting trash washed up on shore.

Some of the random items found on Powell's beaches had been composed into an artsy structure. Driftwood, shoes, buoys, ropes, and even license plates dangled from the arrangement. Added to by visitors over the years, the flotsam montage gradually became a small monument.

The next morning, we were rested and eager to sail onward. Before getting *Angel* ready to sail, I watched *Defiant* with some puzzlement. The ketch's anchor had been raised and her sails were pulling in the gentle breeze, but she wasn't moving forward.

"I'm aground," Bill explained. "You didn't see this." *Defiant* had anchored so close to shore the neap tide had stealthily placed her full keel flat on the bottom. It was a matter of inches, and as the sea returned, a sheepish *Defiant* sailed free, unharmed, within the hour.

Unmindful of callused hands, I stopped wearing gloves to weigh anchor, the wet, rattling chain more easily fed into the deck pipe. Now that the winds had shifted for an ideal sail, I was suddenly eager to get under way. It never takes much for *Angel* to get the best of me and completely kidnap my senses.

7

Key West's Sister Village: Green Turtle Cay

Lust was in the air. Driven by desire, I couldn't undo her zippers fast enough. *Angel* was quickly undressed, sail covers peeled off. We flung ourselves into the windy moment. Mast swaying, bowsprit tossing spray, three taut sails reached for the sun. The rhythmic pulse of her freewheeling prop could be felt through the firm press of her tiller. Like a thing alive, *Angel's* every move was my own for twelve miles of girl-sailboat bliss. Bill, helming *Defiant* just a few boat lengths to my side, appeared to be immersed in the same sailing passion.

Ahead, Green Turtle Cay and its pastel, small island charm lured us in. Some believe that in the early 1700s, feared pirate Charles Vane used the island as a hideout. In the later 1700s, it was settled, as much of the northern Bahamas is, mostly by people with British and African heritage. Elements of both of these rich and interesting cultural backgrounds are appreciated here. Green Turtle also

The next night, Bill and I piled into *Squishy* and visited Randy's power yacht for a movie. The vessel was anchored in the Abaco Sea, just outside of White Sound. While we watched the movie, the easterly breeze freshened to 20-knots, with firmer gusts. Randy was in the lee of Green Turtle, so we weren't concerned.

"Boy, the waves got really high," Bill noted as he was repeatedly splashed in the face just after getting into *Squishy*. Squinting, eyes burning from salt water spray, I struggled to motor back to White Sound. The wind howled and seemed to increase, just for us, while *Squishy* slowly made headway.

I tried to duck behind Bill, but was doused with cold salt water as well. *Squishy* uncomfortably reared up and slammed over each unexpectedly steep wave. I expelled a mouthful of salt water, but it blew back, strand-like, onto my sleeve.

"Damnit!" I shouted.

"What?" Bill said.

"I spit on myself!" I said.

"Say what?"

"I spit– never mind."

"What?"

Slowing, I tried to negotiate the waves with less in-your-face splashing. New Plymouth's faint yellow lights looked too far away. To our dismay, we realized that, during the movie, Randy's yacht had stealthily dragged on her huge, single anchor and reset herself in the middle of the Abaco Sea. After a long, miserably wet ride in *Squishy*, we skidded into White Sound just as the outboard realized it was running out of gas. The next morning, a chagrined Randy replanted his vessel closer to the island.

33

sailed farther south.

8

World Famous Beach at Treasure Cay

Traveling from the north, *Angel,* with her gunkholer's draft, prefers the Don't Rock shortcut, a shallow pass marked by a scattering of lone standing rock islets beyond Treasure Cay's beach. Sand bars do shift here. Bill took *Defiant* through the deeper Atlantic side route around Whale Cay. Concerned about draft, *Escape* took this route as well.

Unprotected by reef and open to the Atlantic's whims, Whale Cay is passable only in fair weather and when there are no rage seas. A rage sea involves curling rows of steep waves that block safe access as they dramatically crash against Whale Cay in explosive geysers of spray. The Don't Rock pass is usually unsafe in the presence of rage seas as well.

In the midst of Don't Rock passage, *Angel* read the shallowest spot at 4 ½ feet, mid-tide. I radioed this find to the others as they sailed around Whale Cay, and they were relieved that they didn't follow me. *Angel's* draft, or depth, is

3 ½ feet. I didn't see the typical sprinkling of grass, shells or starfish below my keel. It was nothing but glittering underwater sand dunes. Because of the sand's pure whiteness, it looked like *Angel* was sailing through a backyard swimming pool. The luminous, turquoise hue over pure sand was so becoming that I wanted to immediately drop anchor and toss myself in. Luffing and loitering to gawk most of the way, I resisted that strange urge.

Past the dark sentinel of Don't Rock itself, *Angel* met up with *Defiant* and *Escape* and we filed into Treasure Cay's deep, dredged channel. Boats can anchor outside of Treasure if there are no strong winds from the northeast to southeast. Completely sheltered inside, the Treasure Cay Hotel Resort and Marina had 150 slips at the time and a handful of moorings in a small, but sheltered basin. For $10 a night, we picked up moorings. It was worth the minor fee to feel secure since the forecast called for a few days of storms and rain.

Tom and Babette were the first to locate the area's two grocery stores and a supply of ice. We followed them into the first grocer and hovered uncertainly over a slim selection of fresh vegetables and fruit. Bill, who was craving a steak on *Defiant's* grill, was disappointed by the scarce pickings. The lone package of ham that Tom found had a pallid, grey cast to it. Squinting at the unreadable expiration date, he gingerly put it back.

Next to the town's grocers, there's a liquor store, café, bakery, and a few gift shops. The most common Bahamian foods we'd encounter on any of the islands are fish, Peas n' rice, mac n' cheese, the biscuit-like johnny cakes, and conch in a variety of forms. Typically cooked with rice, the small and green pigeon pea, or Congo pea, is native to Africa and it's often canned in coconut milk. Bahamian cuisine has strong African influences, and recipes vary from island to island.

Local literature indicated that Treasure Cay was named for the discovery of a fleet of seventeen Spanish galleons that had wrecked off its shores during the 1500s. The ships, transporting their purloined riches, were overwhelmed in a storm. Scattered over the sea floor, a good portion of this lost cargo has not yet been found. It makes a beachcomber want to pay extra attention.

A day later, Bill and I explored the area by dinghy while Tom and Babette spent some time at the beach. Outside and near the entrance to Treasure Cay, rested the jagged, steel carcass of a large shipwreck. I motored *Squishy* up to it and gawked at the unidentifiable rusted shapes. As usual, Bill studied the wreck's shadows for fish.

The nearby Big Lake Creek invited us in for a fascinating, wilderness experience. We'd installed fresh batteries in the handheld VHF, but forgot to bring extra water. Soon, thirst steered us back to civilization and into the Tipsy Seagull's open air waterfront bar. Tom and Babette were already there, looking like characters in a travel magazine as they relaxed in the nearby pool with fruity drinks in their hands.

After we ordered bar food and sat down to eat it, Bill spied a cat slinking along the ceiling's wooden beams. Licking its whiskers, the furry pirate paused and stared down at Bill. Mumbling something about cat drool, he protectively pulled his dinner closer. After staring at Bill for a while, the critter crept away for an easier target.

"This is really fun," Bill said. "I mean, never mind the storms and worries about hitting shallow spots." He finished the rest of his beer, wiped his mustache and shrugged. "I never would've done this alone. I'm getting to appreciate you more and more."

"It's definitely more fun than cruising alone and stuff," I said, cheered that Bill was enjoying my company and appreciating it. Tough, a bit stern, he usually didn't reveal deeper feelings. I also wasn't adept at the touchy feely side of life. It was a funny thing. After a few hundred miles of following each other, weathering storms, and supportively offering help in difficult situations, we'd grown to trust each other. An honest bond of friendship had formed.

However, we were also beginning to feel the expectations and pressures, both social and our own, that opposite gender best friends face. We found ourselves struggling at times, prodded relentlessly by our human inclination for social conformity and by our own boundaries. These boundaries were not set in stone.

While we stayed for a few days and waited for rainy weather to clear, we mingled with Bahamians and boaters. Conversations with mariners typically commenced with sharing of home ports and what kinds of vessels one traveled in. Locals, interested in meeting new faces, told us stories about their families and went out of their way to make us feel at home.

The next day, *Angel*, *Defiant*, and *Escape* simultaneously set sail for Great Guana Cay. Over the VHF, we'd heard fellow cruisers inviting other boaters to a beach side gathering.

9

Great Guana's Beachcombing Surprises

"**L**ook what I found!" Darnell said, triumphantly holding up a perfect sand dollar. "It was just sitting there on a rock." Capt. Pat and Darnell, from Louisiana, were cruising on the sailing vessel *Island Dream*. Darnell's fifteen-year-old niece, Morgan, and her dad, had flown in to stay on *Island Dream* for a while. *Island Dream,* along with a cluster of other cruisers, was anchored over the sandy bottom of Baker's Bay, on the northwest end of Great Guana. The nearby spoil mound of Shell Island and Guana Cay's seemingly endless Atlantic side beach was explored.

Morgan hoped to find sea glass, which are pieces of glass that have been tumbled smooth by reef, sand and surf, and then washed up on the beach. Resembling pieces of semi-translucent candy, sea glass is mostly found in hues of emerald, white, pastel browns, and the less common blue and violet colors. Sea glass with a delicate violet tint is originally from clear glassware that was made prior to the year 1915. This antique glass used to be made with an additive, manganese, which just happened to turn the glass purple after years of outdoor exposure.

Babette, from *Escape,* was one of the lucky ones and stumbled on a rare treasure of the purple kind. Bahamian artisans will incorporate antique sea glass into elegant, high end jewelry, and cruisers enjoy making their own creative works out of the tumbled glass pieces.

Once again I thought about the lucky souls who have found gold Spanish coins washed up on an out island beach after a storm. When the Spanish shipped valuables from Mexico, it wasn't unusual for a treasure laden ship to be blown astray or sunk along the trade route back to Spain. To date, more treasure lies in the sea than has ever been found. About four hundred years ago, pirates and their secret stashes of loot frequented the Bahamas. The sea bound outlaws made Nassau their headquarters for a time. They were such a strong presence an early Bahamian coat of arms reads, "Expel the pirates and restore commerce."

We didn't come across any pirate treasure or Spanish gold coins on Guana Cay, but was still fun to look. Other valuables were found. Darnell and Morgan were admiring a jar full of bright shells. Babette scored a ball of colored rope and weathered driftwood to use for a craft project. I found two attractive cone shaped shells, but when I held them in my palm to show Bill, the shells promptly rolled upright and marched off my hand. Their hermit crab occupants had other plans. Beware of the shell that looks back at you.

Bill found the bottom half of an opaque, olive colored glass bottle that had layers of pink coral growth encrusted on it. We also stumbled upon more enigmatic finds along these remote stretches of out island beaches. There was an abandoned surfer's shack with signs of long ago camp outs; piles of plastic soda bottles and worn out fishing rods with corroded reels. Just south of us, on Man-O-War's beach, a large power yacht was mostly buried in the sand. A victim of a storm, likely hurricane Floyd, only its pulpit rail and an open hatch were visible under an eerie, boat shaped mound of sand.

For the hungry beachcomber, some of the treasures found were edible. The popular coconut palm bears fruit year round. The large green nuts offer mild tasting coconut water and a soft, edible jelly. The more mature coconuts that are starting to turn yellow offer sweeter water and firm white flesh. The challenge is cutting through the fibrous husk to access the coconut inside. Avocado, sapodilla and citrus trees were also spotted in the wild growth inland, and I solicited Bill to help pick a sour orange for use in a cooking marinade.

On the water, traveling boaters found it easy to relate to each other without the prejudices found on land. We discussed the usual topics; weather, anchoring, good harbors, or where to fill the boat's water tanks. Babette contemplated the ideal sun hat with a brim that doesn't flop over your eyes in a strong breeze, and Tom wondered about ice versus refrigeration. Darnell sought input on comfortable cockpit seating while Bill related sailing situations like groundings and the jib that wraps around itself during a gybe.

Adding to the day's amusement, I had to claim *Angel's* runaway dinghy after it floated off the beach at high tide without its anchor attached. Capt. Ron and Terry, from a trawler named *Silk Purse,* had kindly rescued the rubber miscreant after they'd noticed it voyaging, unmanned, into the Abaco Sea. To beach a dinghy, one must always set its anchor high in the sand, or the tide might carry the boat away. Embarrassed, I'd failed to securely tie the anchor, but my friends understood. The cruiser knows how dinghies can have bad moments of Houdini inspired escapes.

On a remote beach, some may just see an ordinary stretch of sand and water. For the boater, it's a gathering place for memorable social activity. Barefoot in the sand, people share their traveling philosophies, or just share anything, while sea glass, shells and driftwood wait to be discovered. Maybe a Spanish coin would be spotted in the foamy surf.

However, we find that the most valuable treasures at these beachside gatherings are the friendships formed with others. These new bonds and the memories of the day can't be bought or sold, and unlike a fleeting material item, they stay with us always.

10

The Joke's on Bill

Today's venture into Great Guana Cay would include an unexpected twist. It began after I picked Bill up in *Squishy* and he stealthily slipped a small, black object inside my beach bag. Our sailboats were anchored in the shallow waters of Fishers Bay, its bottom a mix of sand, grass and kitty litter-like crust. Holding is satisfactory except in strong, southwesterly weather. A few moorings are available for a fee, $15 dollars a day at the time.

When we first dropped our anchors in Fishers Bay the other day, Bill and I had dusted off our dive gear and scrubbed the nascent patches of algae clinging to our boat's bottoms. The water was so warm and clear, we actually enjoyed this chore. The expended dive tanks were refilled at the nearby Dive Guana.

With *Squishy* kept in line by a stern anchor, I tied to the long dock that stretched over Sunset Beach and we walked ashore. A scenic beachside hangout, Grabbers Bar and Grill, was a fine stop for sandwiches. There, in the shade of tall coconut palms, we sat with Tom and Babette from *Escape*. After lunch, the four of us walked down Guana's single road, which curved along the shore of Kidd's Cove, also known as Settlement Harbour. Local lore says that a pirate called Kidd had made this emerald lagoon into his hideout during the heyday of maritime thievery.

Now it shelters the full service Orchid Bay Marina, moorings for boats, and the ferry dock. Overlooking Kidd's Cove is Milo's Fresh Vegetables and Fish Market and Guana Harbor Grocery for basic provisions. Fig Tree Wine & Spirits, a shed-sized pink building built over the shoreline, sells a variety of refreshments and ice. The slow paced, mostly tree covered Great Guana Cay shelters one of the smallest settlements in Abaco's out islands. However, the longish island boasts seven miles of Atlantic beachfront and reefs.

Beach bags slung over our shoulders, Bill, Tom, Babette and I decided to explore that impressive, sandy length. Walking down the road past Dive Guana's headquarters and toward Dolphin Beach Resort, we followed the ocean's fragrant, salty breeze. We could hear the rush of the surf beyond the tangle of tropical greenery.

During a lull in our animated conversation, Bill activated a remote control button hidden in his pocket. The unseen object in my beach bag responded by making a sudden, rude sound. It was the high tech equivalent of the farting whoopee cushion. I hid my face.

Tom and Bab averted their faces, trying to pretend they hadn't heard what sounded like me having serious intestinal issues. Our conversation resumed and Bill pushed the button a few more times. Bab covered her mouth, trying not to smile. Tom gazed at the ground and coughed. They struggled to maintain straight faces. My face wasn't straight at all, and I choked with laughter.

Tom looked up and stifled a chuckle. "No one can have that much gas!" he said. Bab giggled behind her hand. Looking innocent, Bill pushed the button again. I dropped my beach bag and, unable to talk, helplessly pointed at it. We were introduced to the black object hidden in the bag, Bill's remotely controlled, electronic "fart machine."

Energized by the laughter, we left footprints over a long stretch of tawny sand and dipped our feet in foaming surf. Bill's creative prank reminded us that life's lighter side is still accessible in an often too serious world.

Some time later and on a roll, Bill tucked the fart machine into his front pocket and kept an eye out for another victim. He sauntered toward an outdoor eatery that was full of patrons. The electronic toy is sensitive to certain cell phone and radio signals. Naturally, something triggered the box to blast out its realistic noises just as Bill walked past the restaurant.

Some people stared and looked astonished. Others chortled. Dismayed, Bill fished in his pocket, struggling to find the toy's off switch. Followed by laughter, he dashed around the corner, sounding like he'd consumed too many beans. The toy was finally turned off, but it was too late. People were pointing and giggling. This time around, the joke was on Bill.

11

Squid Squadron at Nippers

There's a narrow, dusty path that angles off Great Guana Cay's tiny main street. Signs along this road cheerfully point the way to Nippers. The path is surrounded by lush tropical foliage and mosquitoes. A short walk up a long hill drew Bill and me into this vibrant, tropical party oasis. Built on a steep hill, the uninterrupted view of the Atlantic was awe inspiring. An impressive stairway led to the beach far below.

Bill and I decided to make a day out of this bustling oasis to participate in the famed Sunday buffet and snorkel off the beach. Carrying our gear, we entered the party zone and gawked at the spectacle; neon bikinis, fringed umbrellas, and sunburned people sipping pastel drinks. Servers balancing plates heaped with fries and savory looking sandwiches wove through the crowd. Some people were involved in a limbo contest. Just standing there like a bunch of rubes, Bill and I had no idea what to do next. A troop of sand-caked kids filed up the wooden steps that led to the beach. Laughing and joking, they rinsed themselves under a shower station near the top of the stairs.

"Ahhh! The beach," Bill said, suddenly spurred into motion.

With some longing, I watched a tray of seafood as it was whisked past my nose. "We can work up an appetite snorkeling, then do that buffet thing."

"Geez, those stairs are enough to work up an appetite," Bill said, hesitating at the first step. We pressed against the wooden handrail to let a family pass by.

"Well, it is a pretty big all you can eat buffet." I reminded him.

"All right. Let's go."

The reef just off shore was a visual harmony of life and color. Appreciating the mild weather and gentle surf, we floated over a bubbling, muffled garden of undulating sea fans. Tropical fish darted between knobby corals. Some of the swaying green seaweeds resembled inverted chandeliers, fragile and mesmerizing. Shafts of sunlight danced around us and rippled, rainbow hued, on the seafloor. A small black tip shark swished past. Bill made excited noises into his snorkel and tried to get a better look at the shark.

In the shallows, we encountered a school of squid. They were arranged in a shallow 'V' formation, peacefully hovering in place. Each squid's tentacles were folded together into a streamlined point. Like some kind of living signage, their bodies flickered with soft hues. At one instant, a single squid briefly flared a deep blue while the others responded by flashing a pale, silvery white color. Another squid lazily splayed its tentacles as if it were stretching.

Enchanted, we just floated there, watching. I reached out and the squid squadron smoothly backed away.

Bill swam ahead, hoping to spot the little black tip shark. I drifted over a few empty conch shells. I picked up a weathered shell and peered into its opening. Several sets of eyeballs looked back. As I lowered the shell, two of the occupants swam out and hovered near my hand. They were tiny, rotund fish. They resembled guppies, but were brown in color. I cupped my hand and the two unusually placid fish wriggled in and hid behind my fingers. They felt soft.

I did not expect them to be so fearless. Laughing into the snorkel at how calm these almost comical critters were, I guided them back to their shell. It was not a good idea to be touching the fish, no matter how tame they seemed to be.

Sandy and damp, we returned to Nippers for that much anticipated buffet. While we ate, I swatted at an unidentified insect and missed. In the daylight, with the hill top breeze, there were few bugs. Nevertheless, we couldn't help being uptight about the potential presence of biting pests.

"Hold still," Bill said, slowly raising his hand. "The bug's back, he landed on you." I froze. Bill swiftly smacked his hand on my arm.

"Ouch!" I pulled my arm away and rubbed it.

"Got 'em." He said, pointing at my arm. "There."

"That's a freckle, dum dum," I said, somewhat huffily.

Abashed, Bill leaned over to study the freckle he'd just wacked. "Oh!" He gingerly poked at my arm. "Oh man, I'm so sorry! In this light, it looked like a bug…"

I raised a wad of napkins. "Hmmm, I think I see a fly on your forehead."

Photo courtesy of Dave & Chrissy on Keweloa

12

Today's Forecast:
Exploding Sailboat, Sudden Squall

Despite gray clouds and intermittent drizzle, a 15-knot southeasterly breeze thrilled the contenders in an annual cruiser's regatta. It seemed like an ordinary rainy summer day, until a sailboat exploded. The boat had just crossed the finish line. Sails dropped, the engine was started. As it cranked to life, gasoline fumes in the bilge ignited. The resulting explosion threw everyone overboard.

The boat was enveloped in a blazing inferno of burning fiberglass. Acrid, lumpy black smoke poured into the sky. Amazingly, there were no serious injuries. Swimming away from the blazing wreck, the dazed crew was picked up by other vessels. Everyone in the area was either trying to help or watching the horrifying scene. People were too distracted to notice the rapidly changing skies.

In a solemn mood, race boats filtered into Fishers Bay to anchor. The shallowest drafts tucked behind Delias Cay for the best shelter from potential weather. A regatta spectator, *Angel* followed the others into Fishers Bay. I looked forward to regaining some cheer at tonight's regatta parties. Anchoring *Angel*, I salivated at the thought of socializing over fruity drinks and conch fritters. Uncertainly eyeing the strange skies, I dropped two anchors.

Captain Bill had just finished racing *Defiant* and was returning his crewmember, Dr. Jim, to *Arame*. Jim's 65-footer was anchored in a deeper part of Fishers Bay. I watched with some puzzlement as *Defiant* motored in a circle, but didn't drop the anchor.

"How about heading to Marsh Harbour?" Bill radioed. "The weather looks weird and we're exposed here."

"All right, Marsh Harbour it is," I said with some reluctance. The fruity drinks splashing through my thoughts evaporated.

"*Angel's* on two hooks. It'll take a moment to catch up." I watched *Defiant* speed out of the bay. There was no thunder, but the sky had rapidly grown dark. One anchor weighed and placed in *Angel's* on-bow anchor locker, I grabbed the remaining rode and started hauling. Confounded by the sudden appearance of a fake looking, triangular black cloud to the west, I loosened my grip. The rode paid back out. Long rows of white topped waves reared up and raced toward Fishers Bay.

A cold, wet blast of wind shoved me backwards. *Angel* yanked hard on her single anchor. I scurried back to the cockpit, cursing my dumb luck for not weighing both hooks a moment sooner and fleeing to open seas like *Defiant*. Double curses for not waiting a moment later and leaving both anchors down. Now *Angel* was on one anchor, caught with her pants down between a rock; the storm, and a hard place; the jagged limestone shore.

The winds whipped to gale force and beyond. Unsure if *Angel's* 20-horse power diesel had the strength to overcome such conditions, I didn't unship the anchor line to try and motor away. Raising a scrap of canvas and sailing out unscathed was impossible. Fishers Bay had become a densely packed obstacle course of dragging boats. Using the engine to keep *Angel's* head up and ease the strain on the anchor, I fretted over the sudden lack of options.

In deeper water to the north, a power catamaran capsized, flinging fifteen frightened passengers into the churning sea. The VHF hailing channels jammed with panicked cries. Nearby, a sailboat's instruments read 58 knots of wind just before another vessel T-boned itself on her bow. Through the cold rain and windblown spume, visibility dropped to two boat lengths. I squinted through *Angel's* fogged dodger. A 33-foot racing sailboat directly ahead had turned sideways. She rapidly dragged toward *Angel's* bow.

Crouching low, I dashed forward. Pelting rain stung my eyes and salt spray burned my sun damaged lips. The lightweight racer, *Hawk*, was held off by her crew of athletic, muscular men. *Hawk* slid alongside *Angel*, and again, the burly men held the two bouncing vessels apart. Neither vessel was harmed beyond scuffed paint. A crewman driving a small powerboat struggled to tow *Hawk* away from *Angel*.

As *Hawk* was towed away, her loose anchor snagged *Angel's* rode. Anchor yanked out, *Angel* jerked sideways. Slipping in the cockpit, I fell against the tiller as it forcefully slammed into the new tack. Now the overwhelmed powerboat was unwittingly trying to tow both *Hawk* and *Angel*.

The powerboat nearly swamped. One of *Hawk's* quick thinking crew cut the racer's anchor line. Free, *Hawk* and her towboat fled into a lee. *Angel* fell backwards, her anchor tangled in *Hawk's* abandoned tackle. Watching the limp rode in relation to *Angel's* propeller and glancing at the shore behind me, I gunned the throttle.

Eight nautical miles away, Treasure Cay saw a wind gust of 80 knots. By now, several boats were piled on the shore behind me. Nearby I could see a long-nosed medium sized Morgan Out Island, aptly named *Cyrano*. Composed and cool headed, the couple onboard were motoring *Cyrano* in place to avoid dragging backwards. Likewise, *Arame* had to power in place after Jim noticed her massive, 150-pound anchor sliding over the seafloor. Waves were breaking over his bow. In Jim's experience, the seas have to be over six feet high to accomplish such a thing.

In the Abaco Sea, Bill could barely see *Defiant's* leaping bow as he grappled with vertical waves. He caught glimpses of a trawler nearby, which was also fighting to keep her nose into the howling chaos. Neither vessel knew its position in relation to Delias Cay's coral bar behind them or the rocky Foots Cays somewhere ahead. These hazards couldn't be seen. The trawler and sailboat clung together, assuming the other knew where she was headed.

A shifting gust of wind caught *Defiant's* forward hatch. It slammed open, rain and spray pouring into the cabin. Bill dove below and the ketch's wheel spun out of control. Complicating the situation, an old seal on the hydraulic steering system failed, pink fluid oozing down the binnacle behind the wheel. *Defiant* was bleeding. Fluid pressure slowly dropped, and the sailboat was in danger of loosing steerage. Bill had to act fast.

Guana Cay volunteer fire department and Dive Guana boats were battling the adverse conditions, helping where possible. The Bahamian racing sloop, *Abaco Rage*, had been rafted to her 65 foot mother yacht in the bay. The yacht was now sliding sideways despite two 110 pound Danforth anchors on 300 foot all chain rodes. Unable to motor away, the yacht's quick thinking captain steered toward a patch of sand to avoid dragging into other vessels or into the rocks. Tossed ashore in a jumble, *Rage* was sandwiched between the beach and the leaning yacht. Mast tilted at an unnatural angle, the champion racer looked as if she'd been crushed.

After about 40 minutes of near hurricane force winds, the silt-saturated seas calmed to an oily ripple. *Abaco Rage's* mother yacht, damaged but floating, was pulled free by a diesel powered barge. *Rage* lay flat on her side like a prizefighter knocked senseless in the first round. The wooden boat had not been crushed but did suffer a cracked rib and torn trim.

There were shredded sunshades, broken bowsprits, bent pulpits, and pinched fingers, yet no one had been seriously injured. Thankfully, all 15 people from the capsized power cat had been rescued. The crew from the exploded sailboat was helped out by concerned Bahamians and fellow cruisers. They were provided with donated clothes and places to stay.

Dazed boaters picked up the pieces, and dinghies swarmed about to hunt for lost anchors. Cold, wet and in an odd state of shock, I stared at my painfully cramped hand, which still had a white knuckled death grip on the tiller. In a power struggle with the elements, *Angel's* diesel had managed to prevent her inevitable backwards drag.

People would always ask if I felt afraid in that storm. Afraid? yes! The trick is not to allow this normal human response to degenerate into unproductive panic and interfere with protecting *Angel*. Also, while the storm raged, I didn't have time to consider whether I felt afraid or not. Instant action and decisiveness was paramount. For someone like me who started life by being shy and unconfident, this type of personal control took years to realize.

Regaining our wits, *Angel* and I shuffled out of Fishers Bay. Jim and Constance on *Arame*, as rattled as I was, joined me and we escorted each other toward Marsh Harbour.

The VHF traffic finally eased and I was able to radio *Defiant*. Bill and his ketch were soggy but safe in Marsh Harbour. During the storm, when *Defiant* was blowing sideways, Bill had managed to pour some spare fluid into the steering system. The steering was hastily re-pressurized and *Defiant* maneuvered with her nose into the wind, the confounded trawler still tagging nearby. When the storm's worst finally eased, the two boats had discovered they were comfortably far from the shallows.

Bill was ecstatic to learn *Angel* was unharmed and would soon be anchoring next to *Defiant*. He had no idea how I'd fared during the storm and feared the worst.

"God, I'd thought I'd lost you and *Angel*!" Bill said when we convened in *Defiant's* cockpit. Looking relieved and weary, clothes smudged with transmission fluid, he drooped backwards. His fisherman's sun shirt was torn at the sleeve and his hair was sticking straight up. In one hand, he tightly clutched an empty M&M bag.

"I had no idea what happened to you after you motored out," I said, also slouching in my seat. "It really ███████ We shared each other's stories; how he dealt with driving into the storm without visibility and how I handled being at anchor with a boat dragging into me. We'd been lucky and realized that.

The next day, a new seal kit for *Defiant's* steering system was promptly ordered from the local marine shop. Boaters can order parts and have them shipped in, but must pay an import fee. The parts would take about a week to arrive, so we bided our time by enjoying Marsh Harbour.

13

Abaco's Crown Jewel: Marsh Harbour

Tucked along the eastern coast of Great Abaco Island, Marsh Harbour is the largest community in the Abacos. Not only does the area provide a good, sheltered anchorage, but it's a popular stop for provisions and parts. Upon arrival, when poking your bow around the rocky Inner Point, swing to the left and steam east-southeast to avoid the commercial shipping channel. The layout is easily discernable on the charts.

For boats that are not checked into customs, it's preferable that they proceed to one of the marinas instead of the busy commercial dock. At the fuel dock or in a slip, customs and immigration can then be called in to clear the vessel. Boats anchor in secure holding over the mud and clay-like bottom, which averaged 8 to 10 feet deep in the middle. Free dinghy access was a square wooden raft near the Union Jack public dock. A large dumpster for bagged garbage sat along the road nearby.

Within convenient walking distance from the dinghy dock were food, hardware, liquor, and dive and tackle shops. I also found coin laundry, clothing stores and small restaurants. Many boaters bring folding, wheeled dollies to transport an ample load of provisions while ashore. Restaurant meals, grocery, and consumables are costlier than in the states due to import expenses.

I was thrilled to see soymilk at the grocer, but suffered sticker shock after my bugged out eyeballs bounced into the quadrupled price tag. Diesel and gas cost just under $5 a gallon (at least until the mid 2010s). $10 for a six-pack of beer was considered cheap and it was $5 a bottle at happy hour. Filling the fresh water jerry cans cost me about 20 to 25 cents per gallon.

Taxis can be hailed on the marine VHF radio on channel 6, and they're familiar with the Union Jack dock. Local businesses are contacted on VHF 16, which, as in the states, is also used as an emergency frequency. Boaters in the know hail each other on 68 and then switch to a working channel, usually 69 or 71. While we traveled there, every morning there was an hour long "cruiser's net," broadcast out of Marsh Harbour on VHF 68. This helpful resource for mariners was comprised of weather reports, local events, relevant announcements, restaurant specials and requests for help with things like locating a lost dinghy.

Water based tourists are awed by the Bahamian's amicability and by the fact that boats of all kinds, not just million-dollar yachts, were welcomed. The only truly rude people we'd encountered were a few Americans who were employed in the Bahamas, and some of the illegal immigrants. Boaters from Florida are often tormented in their home waters by marine law enforcement and unreasonable anchoring restrictions. These same mariners are amazed almost to disbelief by the friendlier, more welcoming Bahamian out islands.

The third largest town in the entire Bahamas, Marsh Harbour is a bustling island community with its own unpredictable pace and a single stop light that sways in the tropical breeze. Everyday in Marsh Harbour is an experience. Bill and I arrived in early summer, when local families were preparing to celebrate their heritage with Goombay Time and Junkanoo. The festival grounds in Marsh Harbour overlooked the Abaco Sea. Vendor's huts, a stage, and performers filled the area.

By mid-afternoon, the party started. Children, dressed in sparkling, traditional dance costumes, stepped to a lively Junkanoo rhythm. The littlest ones flashed bashful, dimpled smiles as camera toting tourists captured the precious moment. Adult dance groups joined in, playing bells and instruments.

The festival allowed visitors a chance to experience the taste and beauty of Bahamian culture. Along with daring to dance along, I tried a conch salad that was swiftly prepared before our eyes and had sweet guava duff for dessert. Switcha, a native beverage concocted from limes or lemons, water, and sugar, quenched our thirst. Local artisans sold handmade straw goods for adults and toys for the kids.

In Marsh Harbour, cars rattle by in the opposite lanes than what Americans are accustomed to. Visitors must be careful crossing the street. One balmy morning, Bill and I began a day's excursion with a walk just off Bay Street along the water. Farther into town, we stopped at the Abaco Print Shop, where we befriended Bahamian owner Ruth Saunders and a fabulous lady named Wynsome.

While we milled about in the Print Shop's reception area, the cool, dry air smelling of paper and ink, Bill and I gathered some information about an annual event, Regatta

Time in Abaco. This event was a local tradition, a social opportunity with parties and a series of cruiser friendly races. While we visited with Ruth and Wynsome, a lean, energetic gentleman bustled in and retrieved a box of newly printed newspapers. He politely raised his straw hat and introduced himself.

"Hi, I'm Dave," he said. Bill and I bumped into each other to be the first to shake his hand. We were thrilled to learn that Dave Ralph, and his wife, Kathy, had founded the *Abaconian*, the only continuous local newspaper. With Dave's high energy level and keen mind, it was easy to forget he was in his late 50s. Out of a fondness for his Bahamian home, Dave was a goldmine of local history and we were thrilled to be treated to a personal tour a few days later.

Along Don Mckay, two more bakeries tempted our senses. Three wiry potcake dogs, sniffing the air, were drawn to the scent of baking coconut bread as easily as we were. The town's free roaming pups thrive on handouts and whatever they found in the wild. An abundance of exotic flowers and wooded areas with tropical fruit trees gave Marsh Harbour a fertile, green visage.

"Oh! Oh! Let's stop in here," I said, veering and tugging Bill toward a drug store.

"Hmmm?" Bill said, following me in. Always curious, he browsed while I located a box of tampons, something I'd failed to adequately stock up on for our cruising venture. Shoulder bags full of assorted goods, our legs ready for a rest, we turned toward the dinghy dock. In the magenta haze of a Bahamian sunset, we rode *Squishy* to our waiting sailboats.

The next day, a small group of cruisers from *Island Dream*, *Arame* and *Gusto!!!* pooled together and rented a van. Dick and Carol, a cruising couple from Florida, had arrived on their Island Packet *Gusto!!!*. I joined the group while Bill stayed behind to help our Bahamian friends repair *Abaco Rage's* support vessel, which had suffered damage in the recent Guana Cay storm.

Great Abaco is a long island, about 116 miles of driving from one end to the other. Marsh Harbour is near the middle. This impressive island is mostly covered with pine forest that shelters native creatures like the rare, wild Barbary horse and the Abaco parrot. Touring with the group, I saw where neem is grown and learned about this tree that's referred to as the "wonder tree of the tropics." Later, I'd find Bahamian neem products in the local pharmacies and downtown shops.

The next morning, listening to the cruiser's net had become a challenge. *Angel's* VHF radio speaker faded in and out and was peppered with static. Bill, engaged in his morning routine on *Defiant*, was also listening to the cruiser's net. He learned about a special event and radioed me about it. I was sure he'd just suggested that we attend "snake night" at Marsh Harbour Marina's Jib Room. *Arame, Gusto!!!* and *Island Dream* would be there.

"Er, I'm afraid of snakes," I responded, puzzled.

"Say what?" Bill radioed back, the static increasing as he continued speaking.

"I think I need a new speaker," I said, tapping *Angel's* radio and reaching for the back up, a hand held VHF. I turned it on and heard *Defiant* more clearly.

"...do snakes and speakers have to do with dinner?" Bill was saying, sounding as confused as I was. I imagined his dense mustache and brows tangling in consternation.

I took *Squishy* over to *Defiant* and Bill clarified the matter. He told me about "steak night" at the Jib Room. They also provided vegetarian choices, salads, and home made desserts. Located above the Jib room was Merlin's

Marine Electronics, a little shop that stocked external VHF speakers. I bought one to take back to *Angel* later.

More new friends were made when I shared a table at the Jib Room with Dave and Chrissy, a youngish cruising couple from New Zealand. Straightening his colorful Hawaiian shirt, Dave told me about the momentous night he'd bought *Keweloa*, a Hunter 44 Passage.

"The sun set and I was on the boat thinking," he said with his Kiwi accent. "Millions of stars came out and I could see the Milky Way. It was so beautiful that I lay there on the deck and just got pissed!"

"You got mad?" I asked, confused.

Dave and Chrissy laughed. Waving a hand, Dave said, "Oh no, doll. I got drunk. Pissed is Kiwi for drunk." I grinned. Dividing their time between working and cruising, the couple was involved in a fiber glassing business and before that, they had a hog farm, which was the subject of a number of amusing stories.

"They were food pigs," Chrissy assured us, pointing a neatly manicured hand in the air for emphasis. Bill, who liked bacon, tilted forward. Later, when a live band began to play at the waterfront eatery, the lean bodied pair would be the first on the dance floor. Dave would even spontaneously join the band and they'd hand him an instrument to play, which he would with utmost enthusiasm.

Understandably, Dave was a romantic fellow and would puzzle over why Bill and I singlehanded instead of pooling our resources in one vessel. We'd awkwardly try to explain our mutual interest in solo sailing and how we both loved, and were well established in, our own boats.

Having been raised in a conservative community where alternate ▨▨▨▨ preferences were taboo with guaranteed social rejection, I didn't reveal my personal details. We'd also omit trying to explain a mix gender best

about 'Hooters Patrol' and a crewmember told us that a Hooters calendar shoot was taking place in the area. Well then. That explained a few things.

After spending time in the ever busy Marsh Harbour, provisioning, socializing, and effecting minor repairs, *Defiant* and *Angel* nosed into the shimmering Abaco Sea. A firm, tropical breeze filled our sails. *Angel's* ropes tightened on her winches with subtle creaking noises. Grabbing the wind, she heeled. The tiller pushed firmly against my grip, then eased as *Angel* found her equilibrium. The tilting compass disk steadied in its fluid filled globe. We tacked back in time, heading toward the low, green shape of a most interesting out island.

14

The Man-O-War Cay Time Warp

Back in time, surviving on a chain of remote islands in the tropics required ingenuity. Plaster was made from burned conch shells and wooden boats were built by hand without powered tools. Men headed out in these vessels to earn a living by sponging or to catch common staples like conch, turtle, fish, and lobster. Unpredictable weather was always a factor and sailors did what they could to even the odds.

Smooth, teardrop shaped "thunderstones" were kept on board in hopes of repelling lightning strikes. Technically referred to as *petaloid celts*, these pre-Columbian man made artifacts are rare and surrounded by myth and legend. Shark liver oil was sometimes displayed in a glass jar to serve as a barometer. An approaching storm supposedly caused the translucent oil to grow opaque, warning the men to head for safe harbor. At home, children would gather sea gull eggs, coco plums, and sapodilla fruit to supplement the family menu. Flour, vegetable oil, and sugar were rare commodities until the mid-1900s, when tourism introduced an income beyond subsistence level.

Settled by a single couple about two hundred years ago, and seeing only a slow influx of new arrivals, Man-O-War Cay remained a small, conservative community. Today this 2 ½ mile long island still relies on its own enterprising and independent spirit. Twelve generations of boat builders had established their legacy here and this craft is a thriving business under the Albury name. Two famous Bahamian vessels that grace local waters, *Abaco Rage*, and the exquisite schooner, *William H. Albury*, were built on Man-O-War.

The island's maritime heritage is a boon to traveling cruisers. Mariners can haul out at Edwin Albury's full service boat yard and find supplies at Man-O-War hardware. Albury's Sail Shop originally crafted rugged sails for workboats, but later would turn out quality canvas goods like bags, hats, and jackets. Albury's Ferry provides daily island to island taxi service, convenient for cruisers who are hauled out in the yard.

Visitors can rent a mooring or secure a slip at the full service Man-O-War Marina and dive shop in the island's sheltered harbor. Upon arrival, there was no room in either of the crowded harbors, so we anchored outside. Sails dropped, *Angel* nestled in six feet of water near the northern tip of Dickie's Cay on Man-O-War's bay side. This spot is satisfactory as long as the weather is fair.

"Hah!" I crowed to *Defiant* over the radio, "I beat you by several boat lengths!"

Captain Bill anchored *Defiant* just behind me in deeper water. "Sure. Uh-huh, I just let you win," Bill responded, smug.

"All right, smarty pants. Your boat looks like a giant guppy," I said, Bill and I mirthfully bantering before discussing our plans for touring ashore.

The harbor's main entrance is located on the southwestern side and one must take care when nosing through the narrow channel between the tall lime stone bluffs. Another vessel may be approaching unseen from the inside and there's scant room for two large boats to pass through simultaneously. After clearing the bluffs, to a sharp right is the eastern harbour and to the left is the settlement's harbor with boatyard and marina. We took *Squishy* through the dinghy accessible northern route. This stretch of shallow water leads into the settlement's harbor.

There's a free public dock for dinghies near Albury's Harbour Grocery store. Under the impression we'd just stepped back in time, Bill and I explored the island's two main roads, Bay Street and Queens Highway. A green canopy of branches threaded with vivid tropical blooms arched overhead and birds twittered in the meticulous landscaping. A grandmotherly woman in a golf cart stopped by and tempted us with homemade cinnamon buns for sale. Understandably, her cart was emptied before morning's end.

Tail wagging, a potcake sauntered up, begging for leftover bakery and surveying our ankles with her nose. Potcakes are a small, usually short haired breed of dog popular on the islands. They'd earned their odd moniker for their dishwashing ability. In other words, these pups were skilled at removing stubborn "potcakes," a partially burned disk of rice-based food that's firmly stuck inside a pot after simmering on the fire for too long.

After giving Bill's ankle the wet nose stamp of approval, the little pup attacked him with her tongue. Not a fan of dog saliva, Bill protested and dodged away. I distracted her by tossing a pinch of bakery into the bushes. While our hungry friend raced after it, Bill and I made a quick get away.

Primed by the cinnamon bun lady, we stopped at the Hibiscus Café for lunch. Bill tried to order beer but learned

15

An Exotic Escape in Lubber's Quarters

"**L**ook!" Bill said, pointing at a birdlike creature disappearing into the dense undergrowth, "A penguin!"

I laughed and waved a hand. "Penguins aren't in the tropics." Bill was convinced he'd spotted one. Still laughing, I followed my seemingly confused companion along a narrow path through the small, green island of Lubbers Quarters. This miniscule island is near to the settlement of Hope Town on Elbow Cay.

Boaters visiting Elbow Cay typically make their rounds to Lubbers Quarters for its tree house-like Cracker P's Bar & Grill. Fresh food, social events and an exotic ambiance has put this remote place on the charts. Cracker P's is also the clubhouse and wall of fame for Abaco's legendary wooden racing sloop, *Abaco Rage*.

The healthy minded owner and chef, Patrick Stewart, offers a savory selection of daily specials. After doing a double take over the owner's name, the same as one of my favorite actors, I had difficulty narrowing down a final choice on the menu. I eventually settled for that ever present local seafood, a giant marine snail. Commonly known as conch, this mollusk is legendary for its rubber bandy toughness. However, Patrick used his culinary magic to create an exquisitely tender dish.

After lunch, Bill and I were given a tour of a cottage hidden in the island's tangled tropical foliage. Owned by widely collected fine artist and jewelry designer, Marlee Mason, the cottage was a self sufficient marvel with solar power and rainwater cisterns. We felt lucky to have made friends with her earlier, during our time in Marsh Harbour where Marlee had attended some of the waterfront's social events.

Enjoying her company, we sat on the upper deck and watched her little white dog, Bella, chase hermit crabs in the dense grass below. Bill kept an eye out for his mystery penguin. Marlee shared stories about her adventures on far away shores gathering sea glass for her art.

She was curious about why we had decided to live aboard and cruise, and asked if we'd been influenced by any sailing "heroes." That is, sailors who competed in difficult races or broke world records and such. Lost in thought, Bill and I simultaneously looked down at the ground. I scratched my head.

We weren't into hero worship and we admitted there were sailing people we admired, but we weren't sure about assigning them "hero" status. To me, a hero wasn't someone who sought publicity by engaging in stunts or who tried to make their mark on the world with a man made record.

A preferable idea of a hero didn't cater to the ego, succeed only with the backing of wealth, or seek the spotlight. Bill and I both agreed our personal heroes were the quiet types; people who worked behind the scenes and selflessly took actions that genuinely bettered humanity.

"Einstein sailed," I finally said. "Ah! I have a book by Moitessier, he's awesome for being honest about sharing his adventures. No hype."

Bill was thinking on even more historic lines. "Captain cook, Magellan? Slocum...hmmm–" Bill shrugged. "Did Carl Sagan like sailing?"

Marlee was surprised we weren't following the latest sailing, record breaking thrill seekers. The act of taking a boat around the world was publically glamorized, especially by those interested in profiting from it. Why weren't Bill and I compelled to embark on such an endeavor? We shrugged again and admitted that we lacked the motive or interest.

We didn't need to go far to have fun and we weren't *that* ambitious. Bill has crossed oceans. To him, it wasn't such a big deal. He wasn't thrilled by the time it took, the cost, or by the onerous legal requirements and crooked officials in some foreign ports.

However, a superior debater, Marlee encouraged us to see what she meant about "heroes." After hearing her impressions, I realized I'd been too closed minded. Sometimes it took a strong personality, one who publically sought challenges and difficult goals, to inspire others. People engaged in record breaking attempts, or just anything in the extreme, demonstrate the true versatility and endurance of the human spirit. These valiant souls remind us what we are capable of. That we too can reach for a seemingly impossible goal, learn something valuable, and emerge a better person for it.

Also, it was wrong of me to presume all risk taking, record breaking activity required an excessive ego, strutting vainglory, or a wealthy family. Many people sought difficult goals not to prove anything to others, but to gain a sense of personal accomplishment and a new perspective on life. For these people, succeeding in a challenging race or enduring an extreme sailing environment was an internal thing. It

71

involved self growth and the process of getting to know one's true spirit. This I could relate to.

The sun tracked across the sky and our social visit wound down. Bill and I followed Marlee through the trees and along a coral path to her boat dock. The hyperactive Bella, now chewing on an unidentifiable object, wove around our legs. Bill stopped and made a face while shaking his foot.

"Yuck! I just stepped in penguin ⬤⬤⬤" he complained. "It's green!"

"But penguins can't be here," I said, now with some uncertainty. Marlee stopped and coaxed her dog to relinquish the tattered chew toy. It was a peacock feather. Nose radaring in all directions, Bella swiftly bounded through the grass, seeking more feathers.

"There's your 'penguin,' " Marlee said, chuckling. She held up the ragged feather. Wild peacocks inhabit Lubber's Quarters, their haunting cries occasionally echoing through the hills. Nose wrinkled in distaste, Bill rubbed his stained shoe in the grass. Bella raced over and sniffed the scene, Bill simultaneously trying to dodge the twitchy dog and wipe his shoe.

"Peacock, penguin…" he shrugged. "Why do I always end up stepping in it?"

I grinned and said, "Life can be like that. You get new shoes and then end up stepping into a fresh, squishy pile of ⬤—"

"OKAY, you two!" Marlee interrupted, rolling her eyes in mock exasperation. "Let's go get some dinner."

16

Historic Hope Town

Lubber's Quarters is just a motor-equipped dinghy trip away from Elbow Cay and its main settlement, Hope Town. Enjoying a ride on Marlee's powerboat, Bill and I were returned to *Defiant* and *Angel*, which were anchored in the sandy area near the entrance to Hope Town Harbour. The plan was to jump into *Squishy*, tour Hope Town, and later meet up with Marlee and her friends for dinner.

The channel into Hope Town harbor was 6 to 7 feet deep mean low water at the time and it opens to a completely sheltered area that's about 8 to 15 feet deep. There's no room to anchor between the moorings that have filled the harbor. If available, moorings can be rented. There are marinas in Hope Town with slips, fuel and resort facilities. Dinghies can nose up to one of two public docks, and the Harbour View

Grocery store provides a dock for its shoppers. The settlement also has a bakery and liquor stores. Waterfront eateries have docks for their patrons.

When Bill and I stepped ashore, Hope Town's pastel village, perfectly landscaped and clean, lured us in. Taking the grand tour and meeting the locals, we learned more about this appealing settlement.

Elbow Cay boasts a fascinating past. Just a few years before our arrival, a 600-year-old native Lucayan skeleton was uncovered during a dig to build a house in Hope Town. From what I was able to research, the Lucayans were the first to inhabit the Bahamas in recent history. Likely searching for slaves during his tour through the Abacos, Christopher Columbus described these island people as "well formed, naked and generous."

Sadly, the Lucayans were taken or killed by disease after Spanish slave raiders swept through the islands, and the area was uninhabited for a time. In the 1600s, the English Loyalists began to colonize the Abacos, and Hope Town's tiny community was established in 1785. The British Imperial Lighthouse Service built the settlement's famous red and white striped lighthouse in 1863.

While we were there, this treasured maritime monument still used its original hand wound kerosene mantle and glass prism lenses to guide distant ships. Its antique mechanism was one of three that were still in use in the entire world.

Bill and I climbed the lighthouse's green painted stairs, which wound in a tight spiral. The clunking of our sandals and our breathless voices echoed within the musty, tubular enclosure. Finally reaching the top, we marveled at the gull's eye view. It was amusing to see our anchored sailboats, which resembled ant sized toys, from such a height.

For another nostalgic journey through time, Hope Town's Wyannie Malone Historical Museum shared a wealth of artifacts and curious glimpses into a hard life way back when. I was amazed by the historic dress code, which was incongruous with the tropical climate. Long dark pants and hats were worn by the men, and women modestly wrapped themselves in layers of body hugging fabrics and ground sweeping dresses. Bahamians still possessed a strong sense of modesty and it's wise for visitors to respect local sensibilities.

Bill and I met up with Marlee and her friends that evening at Capt'n Jacks. Overlooking the harbor and lighthouse, this popular eatery served good food and cold drinks on a hot, Bahamian night. Back on *Angel* and ready for bed, I lounged in her cockpit for a while, watching the light house's beam make its timed sweep across the dark sky. The liquid rumble of surf from the Atlantic could be heard on the other side of Elbow Cay. It was a grand thing to fall asleep to.

In the White Sound entrance, on Elbow Cay's southern end, there's Abaco Inn and a marina, Sea Spray Resort. Both serve meals with bar service, and my laptop snagged a Wi-fi signal at Sea Spray. Next to White Sound, on Elbow Cay's southwestern tip, sat Tahiti Beach. This dreamy shimmer of land, fringed with coconut palms and white sand bars, was the place for boat in picnics and kid safe swimming.

On Tahiti Beach, we spent some more time with Marlee and her dog, Bella. The pup bounded up and down the water's edge. The rest of us floated in the warm, clear seas and prodded the sand for sea glass. Considering new projects for her jewelry, Marlee investigated the surf line.

Bill and I made a small pile of sea glass that we'd found. Like eager kids hoping to impress the teacher, we displayed our treasure to Marlee. Legs a blur, Bella raced up and snuffled at our pile, scattering it, her muzzle dusted with wet sand.

Feeling only a little guilty, we spent the entire day posing as lazy beach bums. We drank coconut water, the lemonade-like Bahamian switcha, and snacked on crudely made sandwiches that were partly soggy from the cooler's ice melt seeping into the sandwich bags. The tide came and went.

The hot sun and our inactivity flattened us into a state of lethargy. Even Bella had finally wound down. Waterlogged, gritty with sand, we were ready to return to our anchored boats for freshwater showers and a rest.

17

Wild Island Maze, With Wrecks

Late morning, I anchored *Angel* alongside *Defiant* near the aptly named Angel Cays, a wild stretch along eastern Abaco Island, south of Marsh Harbour. Comprised of several large cays and hundreds of islets intertwined with creeks and shallow bays, the area is a natural paradise.

Smaller boats can slip into the channel south of Snake Cay and anchor in the soft bottom of a small basin behind Deep Sea Cay in 6 to 12 feet of water. Tidal currents squeeze and bottleneck through the channel's mouth at a brisk pace, but once inside, it is a protected hideout from frisky weather. A blue hole in the channel offered interesting fishing and snorkeling.

"I'm not swimming over that!" Bill said, squinting at the blue hole's mysterious depths as we drifted over it in the dinghy. We couldn't see the bottom despite the water's clarity. Here was a dark portal to a labyrinth of subterranean caves that opened somewhere into the Atlantic Ocean to our east.

Many Bahamians believe some of these blue holes are bottomless, and local lore tells of a creature, half shark and half octopus, that dwells in the cave's entrance. The ancients referred to blue holes as the "navels to the earth." Bottomless, earth sized bellybuttons haunted by shark monsters? I decided not to snorkel over this blue hole either.

We poked along in a dinghy safari, our heads swiveling at the tropical flora and exotic wildlife surrounding us. Some 60 species of wild orchids are native to the Bahamas, and glimpses of these delicate blooms were seen. There were a wild variety of tropical trees and cacti. Thick moss curtained over jagged limestone ledges.

Bahamians familiar with the old ways still practice "bush medicine," or healing the body with natural remedies. Surely there were plenty of remedies here. While land abounded with life, the shallow bays teemed with creatures like starfish, turtles, and soft corals. Twittering finches and dragonflies flitted above. Unseen insects trilled in the trees.

The rare few signs of humanity were the enigmatic pieces of abandoned gear left here in 1970 and 1971 by the Owens-Illinois lumber gathering operation on the mainland. A derelict barge with a red barn shaped sawmill sat canted in the shallows, its roof collapsed inward. The remnants of rusted storage tanks and a dirt road were seen on Snake Cay in this remote series of islands.

Nearby in the rocky shallows rested the sunken, angular hull of a large, simple vessel. The boat's entire top half was absent, its hull an empty shell. The remnant of its hand painted name was still visible on the stern. '*VIV…Nassau*' it read.

After losing ourselves in nearly three nautical miles of steamy wilderness, I had to pee. Bill spotted a small dock on an isolated islet. Assuming that it was from the abandoned lumber operation, we pulled up. Scattered in the shallows, clearly seen through the translucent water, were the remains of an antique outboard. The pieces were surprisingly intact, with little corrosion. Mystified, we cautiously stepped ashore, reluctantly leaving the deceased outboard alone.

While my impatient bladder and I dashed into the bushes, Bill found some weathered concrete steps. The walkway rose up a short hill and led to a house that was mostly hidden by tall coconut palms and creeping vines. Of course, Bill just had to investigate. I reluctantly followed, wondering if anyone was home.

"Look, the door's propped wide open," Bill declared, boldly stepping inside. He bumped into the door, its neglected hinges squeaking. The small structure was devoid of furniture and the screened windows were open. It appeared that all work on the house had come to an abrupt halt a long time ago. A broken bag of cement mix lay on the cracked tile floor, the pyramid of spilled grey powder hardened by humidity. Rusted tools and peeling paint cans were crookedly stacked in a corner.

"You could've used the head right here," Bill said, wiggling the flush handle on a pink toilet in an unfinished bathroom. No water came out. "Well, maybe not," he concluded.

Lost in thought, I wondered about the curious island hideout with its pink toilet. Who knew why the place was left open and unfinished. It could be reached only in good weather by a shallow and winding passage through the water. There's no access from land. There were also no conduits for electricity, water or phone lines. Places such as these rely on rainwater cisterns and solar electricity. The largest town in the area, Marsh Harbour, was a 14-nautical mile boat ride away. This hidden house in the wilds surely was someone's dream of a getaway to the real world. Yes, the real world.

Boaters share the same idea, whether it's a sunny day sail or a long cruise to a different shore. It's curious that non-boaters often accuse us of trying to escape from reality. That stubby perspective surmises that the man made realm of TV, traffic, mortgages, ringing phones, 9 to 5 workdays, and computers, which existed for barely 200 years, is the said reality. Thus, that same perspective implies the boater's world of sea, sand, tides, and sun, which has existed for more than millions of years, is not reality or is an illusion.

Of course, the boater knows the truth and embraces it. Both worlds, modern man made society and the natural realm, have validity and experiencing the realities of both can enrich our lives. Balance is the key. Too much of one or the other and we're missing a part of life.

Bill and I left the lone house on the jungle covered island hill and returned to our waiting sailboats. As the summer breeze faded in the night's pale edge, we motored a few miles east and into the middle of the Abaco Sea. *Defiant* anchored while *Angel* pulled alongside for a raft up. We were the only human presence around.

The stark, indigo hush of darkness far from the busy confines of man toyed with our senses. Soon, we noticed things that were before given little regard. High squeaks of a few harmless insect eating bats could be heard. The calm weather allowed the bugs to venture out this far. Rock still on a flat, black sea, it was as if our boats were suspended in space under a glittering symphony of stars.

The difficult to imagine vastness of our own galaxy, its center visible as the Milky Way, blazed across the heavens. Out at sea, the stars are almost bright enough to read by, and streaking meteor sightings are surprisingly frequent. The world and beyond, made small by man's technology, becomes great and mysterious again.

18

Real Life Castaways

One family's unusual history is similar to those compelling fables of castaways making themselves at home on idyllic, coconut palm islands. The real story began in the early 1950s, when the Johnston family's 53-foot schooner grounded on the shallow bars of a remote, uninhabited harbor near the south end of Great Abaco Island.

Fine artists, Mr. and Mrs. Johnston's creative souls were inspired by the area's natural beauty, and they made it their permanent home. The family sheltered in their schooner and in the large caves along the cliffs of the western wall until they finished building a house.

A professor, metallurgist, and an extraordinarily resourceful man, Mr. Randolph Johnston then erected art studios and a foundry to create his now famous cast bronze sculptures. Today, Johnston's son, Peter, and his grandchildren, continue the legacy in this remote oasis.

Remarkable sculptures out of bronze cast in the lost wax process, custom gold jewelry, and fine work from other local artists are displayed for sale in Little Harbour's gallery.

On a quiet summer day Bill and I arrived in Little Harbour with a talkative flock of touring mariners. Dick and Carol from *Gusto!!!*, Pat and Darnell from *Island Dream*, and Jim and Constance from *Arame,* were eager to experience the Johnston family's exotic home.

The open air Pete's Pub, built out of planks and parts from the original 53-foot schooner, sported an eclectic décor of t-shirts, shells, driftwood, and an old, yellow painted stop light. Sandals swishing through the white sand, we bellied up to the little, blue bar for home made food. Lunch was hand written on a board. Burgers, cracked conch, and fresh caught Mahi Mahi were written in as today's specials. Talking and waving at the lazy houseflies that circled our plates, our energetic group absorbed the ambiance.

Arriving boats can anchor in Abaco Sound's deeper water on the outside of Little Harbour. There's a dinghy dock in front of the pub and gallery. Venturing inside the harbor requires a tentative probe through a marked channel and over a sand bar that was 3 ½ foot at mean low water at the time. At mid-tide, it was about 5 feet deep.

Past the sand bar, the pond-like Little Harbour drops as deep as 14 feet, but there's little room to anchor and the holding is questionable. Moorings are available on a first come first serve basis and fees are paid at the pub. Most visitors come for the collectable works of art and stay a short while for island style food and cold drinks. Little Harbour is the last social stop for boaters heading south toward Eleuthera or the Berry Islands.

During Little Harbor's winter season, Pete's Pub frequently holds weekly specials and boater friendly events. The kitchen serves lunches daily, and dinners were served Tuesday through Sunday. Reservations need to be made early in the day to secure a home made dinner. There are no grocery stores or marinas and the area is actually private property, yet the Johnston family kindly welcomes tourists.

Visitors can stretch their sea legs by following the walkway behind the pub. The path leads to a beach that faces the Atlantic and a reef tract called The Boilers. On calm days, SCUBA divers and snorkelers marvel at the reef, its occupants abundant and unmolested by excessive human activity. Just around the northern corner of Little Harbor, in the Bight of Old Robinson, is a hidden island wilderness similar to the Angel Cays with shallow creeks and ocean blue holes.

"There are all kinds of white and pinkish creatures swimming in ocean caves," Fred Davis said. A sailor and professional underwater cave explorer (there were fewer than 100 of these specialized speleologists on the entire planet at that time), Fred described what it's like to dive into the inky blackness of a deep, undersea labyrinth. Built like a wrestler, with short salt and pepper hair fluffed by frequent diving, Fred was a calm, no-nonsense sort of guy.

"There are pale, blind fish with bumps where their eyes normally would be and things wriggling around that look like white centipedes." The small crowd at Pete's Pub had hushed, and everyone nearby was listening with curious fascination.

Fred talked about the time he'd found fossilized bones of creatures like saltwater crocodiles and snakes in Bahamian underwater caves. Dated less than 10,000 years ago, the fossils are a species that no one knew had existed in the Bahamas.

The first one in, Fred explored a new underwater cave site by laying down lines to trace his route and using a compass and computer to map the area. Mexico, Florida and the Bahamas are just some of the places with networks of ocean blue holes and inshore sinkholes.

Sharing his work with the world, Fred had been involved in a film documentary about cave diving and the exploration of new sites. Not as fearless as Fred, I looked forward to experiencing this extraordinary diver's adventures in the safety of a dry, padded settee.

After clumsily dripping ketchup on my shirt, I wandered through a green tunnel of sea grapes to find the washrooms. With doors marked "Pirates" and "Wenches," I made an easy guess and slipped into the correct room. The tall, slender Carol from *Gusto!!!* was in there and we joked like school kids, our laughter echoing around the cracked, stucco walls. Still chuckling, we made our way back to the bar.

Now, stuck in school kid mode, I paid attention to the tradition that visitors participate in by leaving their signatures behind on the Pub's wooden beams around the bar. Like a sentimental youth hopelessly in love with my boat, I glanced about to make sure no one was watching. I stealthily etched a mark into the aged wood:

And then;

Angel + Defiant

19

Touring Eluethera: Drunken Snail Surprise

I didn't see the 20-foot long hitchhiker dangling from *Angel's* bowsprit until Bill noticed. He found it amusing.

"*Angel's* got a runny nose," he gleefully announced on the VHF radio, veering *Defiant* to get a closer look. I hastily untangled the vine-like seaweed, which must've snagged around the anchor when I weighed it. "Boat boogers!" Bill teased. Passing the time by ribbing each other over the radio, we sailed toward a sandy new frontier.

"Welcome to Bryland!" said a native arts vendor soon after we hit shore. Here, Bahamian accents shortened Harbour Island into "Bryland." This three mile long island rests on the eastern side of North Eleuthera. The main approach is from the north along a reef aptly named Devils Backbone. This approach must be made in fair weather and, ideally, in the afternoon when the sun will be at your back. With polarized sunglasses, one can spot the wide, deep blue channel that will take a boat inside the reef. Once inside, a right turn brings you to St. Georges Cay and the Spanish Wells settlement. Local pilots can also be called, via VHF, to render guidance through the potentially dangerous area.

Weather calm and without a pilot, we had turned left along North Eleuthera's shoreline. We cautiously motored past a historic cave and into the sheltered bay to Harbour Island. Boats anchor in soft, grassy bottom near Dunmore Town or tuck into one of the marinas. The dinghy can be beached on the sandy shore north of the government and ferry dock. On shore, Bill and I strolled backwards in time.

"Loyalist Cottage 1797" announced a sign on a tiny wooden house on Bay Street. The oldest church in the entire Bahamas can also be seen here. Golf carts, cars, and giggling kids on bikes slowly rolled down narrow streets. The post office and police station were based in a diminutive and innocent looking pastel pink building. The single room Piggly Wiggly grocery store on King Street was also pink, and its small check out lane used an old fashioned, manual cash register with a bell.

The island charmed us with its slow pace and exotic appeal. Roaming roosters clucked in street corners, while stray cats slunk in the shadows. Typical of the Bahamas, brightly hued homes, profuse tropical greenery, and blooming flowers gave the island a lush appearance. Night blooming jasmine perfumed the humid air.

At first we weren't sure what sort of creature made a low pitched buzzing as a few of them repeatedly blurred past our heads. They were too large to be insects, but in the tropics, who knew? Bill and I were delighted to learn they were humming birds. They were unafraid of us and barnstormed our heads as they sought refreshments in the nearby tropical flora. Evading the tiny birds, we ducked through a tunnel of greenery and down deteriorating concrete steps to access the beach.

"████ girls!" Bill blurted, wishing he had his binoculars. Known for being the hangout for famous models, Harbour Island's eastern Atlantic side beach shimmered in a vast expanse of perfectly uniform pinkness. The sand's soft salmon hue is from nature's inclusion of finely crushed red shells. I dug my toes in the pastel beach.

A woman swam in the gentle surf, the water so transparent that it looked as if she was hovering in the air. Ponies lounged in shaded stables, ready to give tourists an equestrian eye view. I wondered about the pony's beachside deposits meeting unsuspecting bare feet, but a man was herding up every bit of horse poo with a rake.

While the Fast Ferry takes people to and from Nassau, a smaller local ferry taxis people to the nearby Spanish Wells and North Eleuthera's airport. To visit Spanish Wells, cruisers will find deep anchoring along the northeast curve of Charles Island. A dinghy tour past the lengthy waterfront of Spanish Wells revealed a tidy, carefully manicured community and the largest, most well kept fishing fleet in the entire Bahamas.

Dinghy docking was along a stone wharf, so we used it and walked into town. Pinder's Supermarket in Spanish Wells was near an impressive boatyard that serviced the local commercial fishing vessels. Bill was delighted to see a small selection of candy bars, but he didn't find any diet soda. I found onions, but no fruit.

We walked downtown for lunch at the area's main restaurant. The small, quite place had turtle meat on the menu along with burgers and seafood at low prices. Bill asked for a beer, but the server explained that Spanish Wells is a "dry" settlement, meaning no alcohol is sold here. Locals obtain adult refreshments from the shops on neighboring islands.

Typical of small Bahamian communities, the people here were relaxed and friendly. When we were walking along the hilly road leading from down town and toward the boat dock, a local pulled alongside in his car and insisted on giving us a ride to our destination.

The next day we were back in Harbour Island to continue our explorations there. Working up an appetite, Bill and I perused the menus of a waterfront shack, the local equivalent of fast food. The choices were sheep's tongue souse, chicken feet, pig's feet, "boil" fish, or stew conch. Bill eyed a turkey and rice selection with some interest until he noticed that the turkey parts involved resembled beaks, necks, and wattles.

"I'll wait until later," Bill said, looking squeamish. He absently patted the pocket where he normally kept his M&Ms. It was empty. Bill was not into seafood, and neither of us favored random animal body parts. Fresh catches of fish, lobster, crab, and conch are brought in every evening by fishermen. American fare like beef, pork, and dairy is scarce, high in price, and the expiration date of such perishable food was often past due as it sat in the grocer's cooler.

Part of traveling is getting involved in new gastric experiences. By day's end, I'd joined Bill for a cocktail and dinner party in *Defiant's* cockpit. Some of the goods purchased at island stores were imports from other countries and didn't have English on the label.

I bravely decided to try something I'd purchased called escargot. Packaged in a small can, it sounded like and appeared to be some sort of exotic, wild mushroom. Recalling childhood family hunts for morels, oyster, and button mushrooms, I loved these rare fungi and missed the fresh ones from the states.

Bill eyed me over his sandwich and said, "I didn't know you liked little snails." I stared at the black squiggly things in my half eaten dish. I had cooked the suspiciously fishy tasting 'mushrooms' with rice and vegetables.

"Snails?" I said dumbly, suddenly feeling queasy. "Those slimy, little– really?" I hastily stood up, knocking over a cushion. I could handle conch, but not this. My vision blurred and I wanted to retch.

"That's what escargot means," Bill said, his voice a taunting sing song. "Hah-hah, you can't read French!" He tilted sideways, sloshing his cocktail.

When I ralphed over *Defiant's* gunnel, I missed the water. The poor ketch's side looked like she'd been doused with confetti. Snail confetti. At least Bill didn't seem upset. He was laughing hysterically. I was at least coherent enough to feel shame as I hastily washed *Defiant's* side before slithering back to *Angel* and planting my face on her cockpit floor.

Snails mixed with two strong cocktails had been more than enough for my sensitive constitution. Despite occasionally making my own brew, I didn't have the genetics to tolerate alcohol beyond small quantities. It didn't take much to do this lightweight in.

The next day saw a sprightly *Defiant* and a greenish, hung over *Angel*. While I recovered, we couldn't help but talk about our recent tour. Boat boogers, historic places, pink beaches, and drunken snail surprise; it's just another day in the life of a boater.

20

Harrowing Rescues with a Side of Ticks

An old boating friend, Captain James, had asked if we'd like to crew and lend a hand on a delivery trip. Spend a few easy days on his plushy 60-some-foot motor vessel? Why not! However, this innocent ride would take a turn for the worse. James needed to tow four small vessels behind his yacht from Eleuthera and across the deep Northeast Providence Channel to Great Abaco.

The train of vessels to be delivered included a rudderless, heavy wooden sailboat, a 21-foot power cruiser and two smaller center console skiffs. Bill and I tucked our sailboats in a safe spot at a marina and joined our captain friend. Riding a favorable weather forecast, the big vessel was in motion before sunrise. In the ruby glow of dawn, I watched the four boats being towed, in single file from largest to smallest, behind us. We slipped away from Eleuthera and into the open Atlantic.

The ocean swells, remnants of an early fall season cold front, seemed uncomfortably large. Bill didn't like the looks of the skies and his captain's instincts told him it wasn't a good day to be out. However, we were not on our own vessels and would respectfully do what we were told.

It wasn't long before a new wind ruffled the seas, adding to the swollen ocean. Despite her solid toughness, the yacht began pitching and rolling about. Stumbling around down below, I tied the refrigerator door shut, added tape to a banging cabinet door, and rescued a wine bottle as it rolled back and forth across the floor. Today's weather forecast had been far off base.

Unaware that the winds had piped up to 25 knots, I raided the captain's cookie supply. Armed with food, I found a book that had been lying on the floor and wedged myself into a corner. The book was about famous disasters at sea. Unnerved, I got up and found a different read. After settling down again, I heard Bill's voice in the wheelhouse. The rising level of stress in his tone made me look up from the book.

"We've lost the tow!" Bill was saying, "They're drifting away!"

I glanced outside. Only the sailboat was attached to us. Towline broken, the three powerboats were floating away, but they were still tied to each other. They bobbed over the seas, the smallest vessel dipping out of sight behind the waves.

Captain James had an idea. With the awkwardly steep seas, we couldn't bring the yacht alongside the drifting vessels, but we could get close enough for a confident swimmer to jump overboard. He would then climb up the swim ladder of the largest and first boat in the separated tow, *Osprey*, and start its engine. James and I looked at Bill, who had special training during his service in the Navy.

"Oh, ████," Bill said.

Pressed for time, we pawed for life jackets in a dusty locker. Each jacket we picked up was torn, its ancient kapok stuffing falling out. Bill and I glanced at each other, wide eyed. James searched a second locker. So far, he'd found a relatively decent child's size jacket.

"I found another one!" he said. "This is the only adult one that's not ripped. If you don't poke at it too hard, it'll remain intact." He handed it to Bill.

"Uh, Okay…" Bill didn't sound so sure. James and I secured the questionable jacket around Bill, tugging on the buckles and straps. We were careful not to poke it.

Wearing the faded orange life vest, Bill grimaced as he jumped into the Atlantic. Alone in a vast, cobalt blue sea, Bill looked like a doll swimming toward a toy boat. I wondered if he knew he was bobbing in over 12,000 feet of ocean water. Physically fit from his singlehanded sailing life, he cleared the broken lines. After climbing onboard and regaining his bearings, he started *Osprey's* engine.

In moments, Bill had the boat in motion and facing into the building seas, the two other skiffs still tied behind him. In contact via *Osprey's* VHF, Bill struggled over the waves, following the mother yacht in a tense retreat to safe harbor back in Eleuthera. It was too rough for Bill's train to be safely reattached to the yacht.

After a short while, Bill radioed. "We lost *Froggy!*" The towline between *Osprey* and the next boat, *Froggy*, had snapped. Still tied to each other, *Froggy* and the smallest skiff were now helplessly drifting away into the big, blue empty. "Looks like you're next," he radioed to me.

"Copy that," I said, voice squeaking. I fought an awful, sinking feeling. There were no more life jackets!

James retrieved the child sized life jacket he'd found earlier. It was mildewed and slightly torn, but had a closed cell foam interior. It was snug but would do.

"We'll swing past *Froggy* and I'll let you know when to jump," James said, assuring my undersized life jacket was secure.

"Oh, ███," I said. Despite lifelong experience with water and strict swimming drills as a youth, I had nothing like Bill's rugged military background. Never would I attempt such madness unless I was sure it could be done without real damage to my non-thrill seeking hide.

The mother vessel slowly passed *Froggy*. I held my breath. And hesitated.

"Okay, now!" Captain James said, tightly gripping his vessel's wheel.

I plunged into the unwelcoming sea feet first. Saltwater sloshed up my nose. I hadn't jumped far enough and the sailboat towed behind the retreating yacht was pushed by a rearing wave. The rudderless vessel swerved toward me. Howling, I swam away. The sailboat swished past and, fortunately, her path was a narrow one.

Legs kicking awkwardly, I levered like a waterlogged seal over *Froggy's* stern. She bounced over a swell and literally tossed me aboard. My morale plummeted when I discovered an empty fuel gauge. I also recalled James informing me the skiff tied behind *Froggy* had a broken steering system. I had no power. These boats were helpless.

Osprey bounced past and, quick thinking, Bill tossed me the end of a long line. I lunged at the tangle of wet rope. Before it slipped away, I wrapped it over Froggy's cleat. The boat jerked into a new course. I slipped backwards, butt and elbow skidding along the cockpit floor.

The three powerboats united again, Bill resumed towing them to safety. I was stuck on *Froggy*, the boat surfing crazily in a wet, suspenseful roller coaster ride. My skinned elbow burned. There was nothing to rinse off the stinging salt.

After searching the skiff's cooler in vain for a beer, or anything, I curled into a ball on the salty floor. Bill was following James as closely as he could. The most difficult would be negotiating our way past the Devils Backbone and around the coral heads of Egg Reef.

Ten long, soggy miles later, we finally entered a calm, safe spot south of Egg Island, on the west side of Eleuthera. The small powerboats were reattached to the yacht after James dropped his anchor. Dazed and unsure what planet we were on, Bill and I took turns showering and plundering the yacht's bar. I rubbed salve on the raw skin of my elbow.

"Look, another beetle!" I said that evening, flinging the intruder overboard.

"That's a tick," Bill said matter-of-factly.

Moments later, a third tick was found racing toward my leg. Whining I jumped up, slapping my clothing and dancing a jig. James admitted that a dog had been aboard two weeks ago, and ticks were found in its fur.

"How come we didn't find ticks earlier?" Bill wondered out loud.

"Maybe they're brand new ticklets, just hatching after their parents ate the dog and laid eggs in the carpet," I said testily, still dancing. "There could be zillions of them!"

Bill shrugged, unfazed. Grabbing clean bedding, I slept on the sailboat that night. She was a damp, stinky wooden work vessel with no bed, toilet, or living facilities. Also, she had no blood thirsty, skin burrowing bugs. I slept just fine, relatively speaking.

The next day, a better weather window opened, and the captain's charges, including us, were delivered unharmed. Eventually reunited with my sailboat, I gladly resumed a less dangerous, but just as crazy, maritime agenda.

21

Crewing in a Bahamian Sloop Race

The striking scenery would curl anyone's sails. Great stretches of Eleuthera's eastern shore consisted of stone cliffs that angled straight into the sea. Even in fair weather, the Atlantic's restless swell crashed against the jagged facets in sonorous, hollow sounding blasts of spray. Swish-POW! After each mighty crash, foaming seawater trickled down the weathered surface in a white laced network of waterfalls. At sea level, the cliffs were rough with numerous caves. Swish-POW! Damp, briny air tickled my nose. Now I understood how those caves were carved into being.

"Can you imagine what this place looks like in a storm?" Bill mused. *Defiant* and *Angel* weren't planning on finding out. Instead, we sought safety back in the bay and stumbled upon a Bahamian sloop regatta. Throughout the Bahamas, traditional wooden workboats sparred for top honors in a series of national championships. Late summer, Eleuthera hosts one such regatta in its sheltered northern bay.

Harbour Island became the bustling center for awards parties, street vendors, and festivities. Representing various Bahamian island locales, the crews from both the class A boats, at 28 feet in length, and the 21-foot long class B sloops, gathered at Valentines Marina on Harbour Island. The ferry disgorged crowds of race fans, along with teams from the Nassau based TV and radio stations.

Bill and I met up with a group we'd befriended earlier from Hope Town in Abaco. This enjoyable group crewed and cared for the class A sloop, *Abaco Rage*.

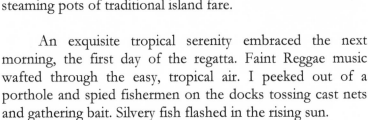

We followed them through Harbour Island's regatta street fair. "The Pineapple, fruit n' veg," announced the wooden sign at a diminutive fruit shop on Bay Street. A vendor's stand called "Dis-we Ting" sold sweet coconut water and seafood specials. Perspiring over portable stoves, Bahamian cooks stirred large, steaming pots of traditional island fare.

An exquisite tropical serenity embraced the next morning, the first day of the regatta. Faint Reggae music wafted through the easy, tropical air. I peeked out of a porthole and spied fishermen on the docks tossing cast nets and gathering bait. Silvery fish flashed in the rising sun.

I joined Bill and the *Rage* crew for a stroll into Dunmore Town for breakfast. While the local resorts offered great food and glitzy ambiance, we went off the beaten path to seek out the native mom-and-pop establishments. Angelina's Starfish, north Dunmore, was popular with the *Rage* crew. We also investigated Harry O's, a tiny take-out shack near Fisherman's Dock and overlooking the bay. There was no seating at Harry O's except for a few stools in front of the shack.

After breakfast, it was time to race. Midmorning, the winds became gusty, bringing summer showers.

"We'll need extra people for this," said Stafford Patterson, his eyes taking in the changing skies, then settling on Bill and me. The race rules allowed a limited number of foreigners as crew. That afternoon, Bill and I were sitting on *Abaco Rage's* beamy deck for a crash course in Bahamian sailboat racing.

The sloop regattas evolved from fishing boats racing each other to be the first ones in port. The first boats secured top dollar for their catches. Those unofficial races evolved into official regattas without the cargoes of fish. Race records began in 1954. True to the original workboat's spirit, race rules prohibit modern equipment. There must be no engines, winches or wind vanes. Sails are canvas, and the hull and spars are wood. The boats themselves are built by hand with skills and techniques passed from generation to generation.

Over time, the race boats evolved disproportionately huge mainsails with narrow, vestigial jibs. *Abaco Rage's* hull was 28 feet long, but her mast reached an impressive 65 feet in height. These overpowered sloops required large crews. Capsizing was a strong possibility should crewmembers slip off the pries or if the mainsail wasn't immediately depowered.

The pries are narrow wooden boards that are slid across the deck to protrude far beyond the windward side during each tack. Crewmembers had to shimmy under the low boom while tacking. The pry would be hastily shoved to the deck's other side. As the vessel settled into her new tack, the crew slid their butts onto the pry, tightly clinging to it and each other. Such an endeavor took teamwork and balance.

Competitors started from an anchored position.

"Every ting to starb'd," instructed the race committee. A hat was held in the air. "Heads up!" As soon as the hat was lowered, six anchored race boats hustled to life.

The *Rage* crew hauled the grapnel anchor onboard while simultaneously raising the sails. A sudden wind shift caught us, and *Rage* twitched perilously. The tips of her pries, and the people on them, were momentarily dunked into the water. Someone squawked and a shoe floated away. Everyone hung on and *Rage* righted. We surged ahead and tried to catch a newly built wooden sloop from Andros called *Red Hot Thunderbird*.

"It's odd seeing your keel while sailing," said *Rage* crewman, P.G. LeBoutillier, as he perched on the end of the middle pry. I glanced at *Rage's* blue painted full keel, easily seen as we hung over the clear water. It felt as if I were on a see-saw.

"I could dive up crawfish here," Colyn piped up. Aside from crewing, the affable Bahamian enjoyed cooking for the *Rage* gang.

"You think that cloud's coming?" someone asked. Heads turned toward the sky, where a dark squall line was brooding over the bay's northern end. It barely seemed to be moving until it was upon us.

"Drop the main!" cried the helmsman, Jeff Gale. Rival boats scattered like leaves in the sudden wind. *Rage's* anchor was lowered and I helped control the flogging mainsail. The red-hulled *Silent Partner* veered past, struggling with a stuck jib. Rival boats rushed over to help.

Waiting for the rain to pass, we huddled inside *Rage's* damp interior while beers and bad jokes made their rounds. The little squall soon subsided and the regatta began anew. Spirited sloops were bristling for a good battle, but the winds had faded after the rain.

"I've never seen *Rage* sailing backwards," Stratton observed.

Colyn wistfully gazed into the water and said, "I could dive for crawfish and swim back to *Rage*." The triangular racecourse was shortened, and *New Southern Cross* drifted into first. We came in third.

The next day brought new racing adventures, especially for Bill. For breakfast, he couldn't find his usual favorites, so he'd settled for something different. It would catch up to him later.

After eating, we joined the *Rage* crew as they clustered together, discussing strategy. A skipper from a class B sloop approached and appealed for a crewmember. Since the winds weren't as strong and *Rage* didn't need the extra ballast, Bill was snagged.

"But..." said Bill as he was whisked down the docks. The smaller 21-foot sloops had names like *Ant's Nest*, from Ragged Island, and *Lady Nathalie*, from Acklins. An aggressive fleet, they'd often sail so tightly that crews literally had to untangle the boats from each other.

Bill served well until his stomach had an untimely mutiny over this morning's mystery breakfast. The sloop had no toilet. While the boats waited at anchor in the bay for the next race, Bill pondered his dilemma.

"What do you do if you really need to, uh, you know?" Bill asked, awkwardly clutching at his cramping bowels.

Sympathetic, yet amused, the captain said, "We jump in." Mortified, Bill had no choice but to slip into the sea and slink far away. Of course, the large cluster of idle sloops knew that he wasn't out for a leisurely swim. They pointed and laughed as Bill swam back, looking green.

"Whatever I ate, I won't eat it again!" Bill vowed after he returned to the docks and relayed his unpleasant story. Clothes wet, hat and mustache drooping, he looked a mess. Unable to help it, we were howling with laughter.

"Is there no pity?" Bill said, grumbling and trying to smooth his salted, mussed up hair. A beer was pressed into his hand and he was reassuringly clapped on the back.

"But, you didn't dive up crawfish while you were there?" Colyn asked innocently. Bill feigned a withering look, and the good natured gang broke out into more laughter. It was just another day at the races.

22

Crash Course Cruising Lesson

Running aground is a drag. When flying downwind in a firm 18-22 knot breeze, hitting bottom is outright scary. It was November, and the winter season's cold fronts were starting their blustery cycles. We had to return to home port and resume our working lives for a while. *Angel* and *Defiant* left at sunrise for a day's 56 nautical mile run from Green Turtle Cay to Great Sale Cay. The out islands passed by swiftly and we were already nearing Carters Cay Banks by the afternoon.

There was no way to turn my cutter rigged boat in time. I could see the sand bar rush up and, THUNK! *Angel's* keel plowed into a mound of sandy silt. Startled by the abrupt halt, I stumbled and stubbed my toe. The frazzled sailboat, luffing now, rolled upright and began pivoting on her keel. Sheeting in, heeling over with the sails, I slid from the sand bar. I was free! Then, *Angel* abruptly bounced into a larger one.

The sailboat surrendered to the falling tide, her depth sounder now taking notice and displaying those unhelpful two dashes. I doused sail. It wasn't practical to try and set anchors for kedging off; *Squishy's* outboard was secured in *Angel* and rowing an inflatable in 20 knot winds is futile. I wasn't up to the rugged idea of swimming an anchor out on a floating fender. I'd rather wait.

The grounding might make a dramatic barstool story, but in truth it was as dangerous as tripping into a feather bed. A shoal draft boat with a wide, flat bottomed keel, *Angel* habitually flirts with soft shallows. For common sense's sake, we do give coral heads, reefs, sponges, and thick sea grass a generous berth.

"Not again!" Bill lamented. *Defiant* wanted to help, but nothing could really be done. *Defiant's* deeper draft couldn't get close enough without compromising Bill's own safety. The simplest plan was for Bill to continue to Great Sale. I planned to catch up when the tide freed me some time later. Reluctant, Bill sailed on, uneasy about leaving me and *Angel* alone and in such a vulnerable state.

After *Defiant* disappeared over the empty horizon, anxiety gnawed at the edges of my thoughts. Far from human activity, I saw no other vessels. Suddenly, the solitude wasn't so nice. I hailed Bill on the radio. Negative contact. Too uneasy, I didn't do much except pace the tilted deck. A thunderstorm formed nearby.

Two hours passed and *Defiant* turned into Great Sale's northern tip. So far, Bill had been unable to raise *Angel* and the silence unnerved him.

"*Angel, Angel?* *Defiant*." No response. *Defiant* swayed, toying with the idea of turning around, but the setting sun would make a safe search impossible. Bill had just watched a thunderstorm pass over *Angel's* last known position.

That ill weather and the mysterious radio silence compounded his unease. Motoring, reluctant to drop anchor, *Defiant* swerved to and fro, not sure what to do. Oddly, *Defiant* was the only vessel there, restlessly circling in Great Sale's western bight.

The island offered good shelter on its west and east sides, depending on wind direction. Bill finally anchored near a low spot with a clear view of the seas in *Angel's* direction. This allowed him to scan the darkening horizon with binoculars and watch for *Angel's* navigation lights. A few times, he heard *Angel* calling on the radio, but when he responded, all he got was silence. Other than that puzzle, there were no signs of his lost partner. *Defiant* was alone.

Angel's nemesis, Carters Cay Banks, is a series of shallow, sandy bars near a common route to and from Little Abaco Island. The charts can't keep up with this shifty piece of seascape and eyeball navigation is necessary. In the clear seas of the Bahamas, navigators read water depth by its color.

One way to become familiar with the water depth and color relationship is to explore in the dinghy and sound the bottom with a boat hook or leadline. Pale tan, brown, sandy white and light green shades are shallow. Shallow grass appears as dark green. The emerald greens and rich blues of deeper water are found to the southwest of Carters Cay Bank and boats can easily avoid making *Angel's* blunder. The bank is clearly seen and, no excuses, I was sailing too close and wasn't attentive to the water's changing color until it was too late.

A nearly full moon rose like a yellow bubble over the Abaco Sea. The water glimmered. There was enough illumination for a weary *Angel* to shuffle onwards. The tide had buoyed us free at sunset, and we fled for deeper waters. The squall that had passed through earlier had done no worse than drop cold rain.

I hailed *Defiant*, but there was no response. Suspicious of my recently installed external speaker, I tried *Angel's* spare VHF and antenna, and then the handheld. The airwaves were mysteriously silent.

With Carters Banks at my stern, finally, the night sail in this particular area posed no hidden danger. The only hazard was the stretch of water from Sale Cay Rocks to Little Sale, which could be seen and avoided in the moonlight. Feeling safer at a slowed pace, I dropped a headsail and turned on the diesel. Its strong purr was reassuring while I tiptoed through a stark world of inky waves and an otherworldly late November moon. It was a long, spooky run. When I neared Great Sale, I could see a light.

Angel couldn't move fast enough when her bowsprit rounded the corner of the calm anchorage. There sat *Defiant*, lights ablaze and waiting. Two relieved boaters were finally reunited in a fit of attempted raft ups and insistent chatter. At last, all was well.

"I couldn't help but worry the whole time!" Bill said, nearly angry at me for causing him such a state of anxiety.

"I was trying to shave off some miles," I explained, abashed, looking at my feet. "Bad shortcut."

"Well, stop running aground!"

"Okay."

Using my diving gear, a daylight inspection of *Angel's* keel revealed no harm but for some lost bottom paint. As far as the radio communication conundrum, Bill discovered a broken microphone button on his VHF. *Defiant's* radio could receive, but had not been transmitting Bill's calls.

We'd been effectively cut off from each other due to my graceless grounding and by one little plastic button as it succumbed to the squeezing grip of a worried companion.

23

Crossing To Lake Worth, Florida

Poised to cross the Gulf Stream, we'd spent the night anchored over Barracuda Shoal on the edge of Little Bahama Bank. Under the purple blush of dawn, I weighed anchor. As sailboats seem to do, *Angel* began to fidget like an excitable canine just before a walk.

After I pulled in most of the anchor line and fed it into the deck pipe, *Angel* impatiently skittered sideways, dragging a length of chain and an upended anchor along the seafloor. Coffee spilling, I cursed. *Angel* bounded away while I scrambled into action. The frisky canine had streaked away with the leash.

Bill and *Defiant* had a rougher start. Puzzled, I watched *Defiant* motor away from the empty anchorage with a strange limp. She drifted to a stop, brownish black smoke pouring from her exhaust. An oil pressure alarm wailed.

"*Defiant's* stroking out! I'm stopping," Bill radioed. The ailing sailboat drifted backwards, her engine briefly running away before Bill could shut it down. When *Defiant* was securely anchored, I pulled alongside and rafted up.

"Oil pressure's dropped and the crankcase level is a bit high, but there's no water in it. I know I didn't overfill the oil." Bill informed me.

I scratched my head and said, "Running away, smoking like that, you know she's eating it. Does the oil smell like diesel?" Bill ducked into the engine room and returned with a smudged nose.

"Can't tell. The whole thing stinks like diesel." He looked forlorn.

"You have internal fuel lines?" I asked.

"No," Bill said, brows plunged downwards. "HAH!" He blurted, realizing what was wrong. He scrambled into action while I stood by and handed him tools.

Defiant's engine used a custom added electric diesel fuel pump, but the old mechanical pump was still in the system. The aged pump's diaphragm had developed a crack, which allowed diesel fuel to seep into the oil. When enough fuel contaminated the oil, it raised fluid levels just enough for the engine to burn the excess and briefly race out of control, coughing up dark smoke. The diesel intrusion also changed the oil's viscosity, which explained the dramatic plunge in oil pressure.

Defiant's health was restored in a few hours. Bill had drained the bad oil and replaced the fuel pump with a spare. It was late morning, not too late for a day's crossing, but we were cutting it close.

Sails finally raised, catching a good breeze, we left the relative shelter of Little Bahama Bank. Angling in the Gulf Stream's strong current, we headed toward the Palm Beaches on Florida's east coast. *Angel* and *Defiant* planned to hop south along the coast, anchoring at night and sailing by day.

After the rough morning, I was grateful for an uneventful crossing. While *Angel's* tiller pilot did most of the helming, I plotted my position on a paper chart every hour as long as I could see land. After that, it was a rough calculation of speed, bearing, and the affects of current. When I went below for a snack, I forgot to unclip the safety harness and was jerked to a halt, outstretched arms flailing while I teetered just out of reach of the galley.

Things became more interesting when *Defiant*, about a mile ahead, spotted a hazy blob on the horizon. The blob hailed him.

"...this is US Naval warship...." The ship had relayed *Defiant* and *Angel's* bearing, speed, and position before politely introducing itself. The warship suggested we shift a few degrees to starboard to assure safe passing distance. Awed, we respectfully obliged. The big, grey ship passed, bristling with antenna, guns, and other official pointy things.

The Palm Beaches and Lake Worth inlet is a hot spot for boats coming in from the Atlantic or exiting the ICW. With our delayed start, we'd be arriving after sunset and as evening fell, I worried about finding the inlet. Numerous freighters roamed through the inky, clouded night. Though they blazed with lights, accurate distances and speeds were difficult to determine in the dark.

Nearing Lake Worth, I couldn't discern the inlet's lighted buoys from the dazzling confusion of the populous Palm Beaches. Blinking signs, billboards, moving car lights, street lights, and boat traffic triggered an eye watering sensory overload. *Defiant* had her own uncomfortable moment when a large patrol boat raced up and rudely studied her with a spotlight. Bill's night vision was ruined. To Bill's relief, the patrol vessel lost interest and gave *Angel* a cursory sniff.

Groping toward the inlet's general vicinity, I watched for other boats that might duck in or out of the unseen channel. Soon, a brightly lit gambling vessel exited Lake

Worth and revealed the inlet's location. Lagging behind *Defiant*, *Angel* finally wandered in.

I turned to port and entered the lake's southern half. After releasing the chain stops, *Angel's* anchor rattled over the bow roller and splashed down in only one fathom, six feet, at low tide on soft bottom. Lake Worth is mostly shallow and its dredged channels are marked. There are deep pockets in the lake's southern half with ample swinging room.

The next day was set aside for provisioning and resting. A Winn-Dixie grocery store was located near shore on the Riviera Beach side, just north of the fixed 65-foot high bridge. The only dinghy access we found was at the Municipal Marina on Riviera Beach, which was due west of Peanut Island. The dock fee was ten dollars per day. Here, we found gas, diesel and helpful information. The Municipal Marina is just a few blocks away from the Winn-Dixie.

After six months of island hopping, our perspectives had been altered. The seemingly infinite rows of densely packed isles in an American grocery store had us awed and even unnerved. Bill resisted immersing himself in the vast selection of various flavored M&Ms. I kept staring at the perfect fruit displays, where nothing was wilted or moldy. While so many people were struggling and starving in our world, this ostentatious display was disconcerting. Bill and I felt as if we'd just dropped in from another planet.

Another thing we immediately noticed was the impact of television. While seated in an eatery with TVs over its bar, we were dismayed by our reaction to it. After going so long without seeing television, aside from the rare movie in Bill's collection, we were appalled by it. Television was noticeably violent. We had to once again be desensitized by TV's constant presence in order to accept the remarkable levels of severity and violence it regularly portrayed. If we could've afforded it, we would've dashed over the Gulf Stream and back to the more palatable reality of the islands.

The ICW in southeast Florida can be extremely crowded on winter weekends. Tidal current and nearly nonstop boat wakes stir up a steep, rough chop even when the winds are calm. Weather permitting, it's easier for a sailboat to travel on the outside to avoid heavy traffic, the wakes, and the numerous bridges.

We did just that. In the muffled calm before sunrise, *Angel* and *Defiant* headed into the Atlantic and nosed south. We left Lake Worth and sailed toward Miami.

24

Coastal Atlantic:
Lake Worth to Biscayne Bay

Lake Worth astern, *Angel* and *Defiant* had just slipped into the Atlantic and headed south. The Palm Beaches were still asleep. It was Sunday morning before dawn and we were the only boats moving in the dusky, serene moment. *Angel's* three sails were embraced by a humid ten knot breeze as she waltzed a rolling Atlantic swell. Halyards clinking, *Defiant* deployed all three sails as her ketch rig reached for the wind.

To reduce the Gulf Stream's counter productive effects, we hugged the coast at a depth of about five fathoms and less. The northerly flowing stream can be felt close to shore along southeastern Florida.

Tiller pilot engaged, *Angel* helmed while I scattered a few crumbs of food on her bowsprit. The gesture of feeding *Angel* was part of an old ancestral tradition to show respect and acknowledgement to the vessel's spirit. Along with sensible seamanship and preventative maintenance, I clung to my family's superstitions. *Angel* is my lover, an active partner in the adventure of life, as opposed to being a mere object that's casually used as transportation. I was certain that I wouldn't bond so deeply with something that wasn't endowed with a soul or some kind of inexplicable energy of its own.

At least I wasn't alone. To this day in the West Indies, mariners feel that a boat must have her own spirit to be successful and safe. Sometimes, an animal is sacrificed for that cause. In parts of Scotland, fishermen sprinkle new vessels with whisky, barley, and bread. Ages ago, the Vikings tied slaves in the path of a new ship before it was launched. Crushed by the ship as it slid into the sea, the hapless slaves supposedly transferred their souls into the boat.

Blood and gore soon gave way to symbolic red wine and then to the American's sparkling beverage christenings of today. Also, boats around the world are traditionally referred to as "she," and in some countries as "he," instead of "it." While cruising, I'd frequently notice other skippers talking to their boats or offering Neptune, sometimes the boat herself, a share of rum. Maritime traditions run strong.

After a hot sunrise, Florida's inlets soon resembled beehives with frenetic swarms of vessels randomly buzzing in and out. The tranquility was shattered. Adding to the growing clamor, *Defiant* and *Angel* turned on their diesels and motor sailed to maintain reasonable speed in the increasingly mild conditions.

"Are those guys following you?" Bill radioed.

"Uh–oh!" I blurted, startled by the parade of boats closely trailing *Angel*. I hadn't heard them sneaking behind me. Fumbling about, I put my clothes on and, peep show over, the nosey vessels meandered away.

Soon, we passed Boynton Inlet with its low, fixed bridge. Sailboats could not enter here. Next was Boca Raton

Inlet and Hillsboro Inlet and both have opening bridges for sailboats to access the ICW. It's always wise to note the nearest safe harbors along one's planned route should the weather turn.

By mid afternoon, we approached Ft. Lauderdale and it was the most chaotic channel we'd passed so far. My grip on the tiller tightened. I stood up to steer instead of sitting. Overhead, a blimp continuously circled in the sky. Its slow, rotund shape was a stark contrast to the visual cacophony of angular high rises and tower cranes that dominated the coast. The droning noise of airplanes was nonstop. Dodging the ceaseless boat wakes, we plodded onward. Miami's yellow haze enveloped bulk rose over the horizon.

Defiant rooted along Miami Beach for ▓▓▓▓ sightings while I stayed on the rhumb, the boater's straight line to the next waypoint. I was too weary and lazy to divert course until a jet ski dumped its lone jockey in *Angel's* path. I swerved in a sail flapping panic. The rider splashed after his drifting craft.

Once I was certain the man was safely reattached to his jet ski, I reigned in *Angel's* sails, hurrying to catch up to *Defiant*. At Miami's bustling Government Cut, we paused with throttles pulled back and sheets loosened, our sails slowly flapping. We waited like cars at an intersection for two behemoth cruise ships to slowly steam out to sea. It was then I wished *Angel* possessed a horn.

The sun fell behind Virginia Key. In the deepening twilight, I aimed for the flashing light at the single entrance to the Key Biscayne and Cape Florida channels. I'm easily overwhelmed by the confusion of urban artificiality, but feel at ease when sailing in wild, natural places. It felt good to be away from the clutter.

Finally relaxing, I inhaled the fishy air wafting from Biscayne Bay's tidal flats. It smelled like low tide. This serene place was free from the sense stunning din of a city. *Angel* led the way into the straight, deep and wide Key Biscayne channel, her spotlight finding each unlit day mark. We also found something else.

"You see that?" Bill radioed. A massive, spidery shape leaped into the spotlight's narrow beam.

"There," I said. Perched on long stilts, a triangular structure emerged from the shadows.

"Stiltsville!" Bill exclaimed. Along the channel's edges were the funky remains of several fishing and vacation cottages, which were built high over the water. Known as Stiltsville, the structures were presently abandoned. Wandering into Biscayne Bay, we anchored out of the way of mosquitoes and the night fishermen's travel routes. *Defiant* and *Angel* were finally at rest after a 68 nautical mile run from Lake Worth.

Alone in the darkness, we could see Key Biscayne and the Cape Florida lighthouse on the island's southern tip. The oldest light in the state of Florida, it first began guiding ships in 1825. Key Biscayne offers anchorages, a marina, and dinghy access at its northern end. There's anchoring for a fee in the sheltered No Name Harbor. There are also restaurants, provisions, and over 400 acres of the scenic Bill Baggs state recreation area.

Back in the Florida Keys, our travels ended for the season, but by now we were thoroughly addicted to cruising. Highly motivated, we returned to our working lives and budgeted for the next year's seasonal sailing adventure. Bill took people fishing as he'd always had. Inspired after our travels, my paintings took on more variety and color. To supplement the unpredictable artist's income, I wrote articles about our travels for various boating magazines.

A number of those articles appeared in *Southwinds Sailing Magazine*, a monthly publication that focused on boating in southerly waters. There's something ultimately appealing about sharing a story with others, and encouraging them to give boating, in any form, a try. I also liked to share my mistakes, no matter how embarrassing, so others could avoid the hassle of making the same ones.

The editor of *Southwinds*, Steve Morrell, has his own collection of riveting sailing adventures under his belt. I knew that he'd cruised throughout the Bahamas in an engineless 27-foot Folkboat named *Trifid*. Afterwards, the vessel starred in that zany movie *Caddy Shack*. I can recall those humorous scenes where actor Rodney Dangerfield's pushy powerboat kept picking on Ted Knight's little sailboat. The apparent damage done to *Trifid* was faked for the movie. No boats, power or sail, were actually harmed.

25

Cruiser Interrupted:
The Do-It-Yourself Boat Yard

Eventually, every cruising boat owner must interrupt his or her sailing life for a date with the boatyard. The occasion isn't pleasant. First, one's beloved vessel gets plucked out of her element by a couple of straps. Exposed and vulnerable, *Angel's* dignity disappeared as she was scooped over dry land, her portly figure unceremoniously propped up by stands. Once powerful, lively and incessantly fidgety, she was now helpless and still. Enhancing her comatose appearance, the anchor locker drain under her bowsprit oozed a slimy strand of stagnant water. *Angel's* ability to drool added to my discomfiture.

Dripping, whale like, *Defiant's* blue figure was slowly raised out of the water by the marine Travelift, swung over land and blocked up next to *Angel*. Feeling like fish out of water, Bill and I stood there, staring at our boats. I scratched my head. Bill absently pushed at the wrinkles in his fishing shirt, and then crossed his arms.

Out of the water, our vessels looked massive and utterly helpless. I was surprised to see that Bill appeared as daunted as I was. It was early fall, a time we hoped wouldn't be too hot for the drudgery ahead.

"Well," He said. "Hmmm." He tugged his hat off and slapped it back on.

"Uh–huh," I said, scratching my head again. I twitched my slightly sunburned nose. The hot, dusty air carried that indescribable boatyard bouquet of diesel, solvents, and pungent metallic bottom paint.

"Well," Bill repeated, sighing. He reached into his front pocket for a bag of M&Ms.

After some more hesitation, candy munching, and gravel kicking, we finally got moving. Bill went up to the boat yard's store for supplies and I trailed along. Reading and studying how to do a fiberglass boat's bottom job was different than actually doing it. I was glad to follow Bill's lead. We'd hauled out on Stock Island, the northern part of Key West. The boatyard, which isn't there anymore, was known as Peninsular and at that time boat owners were allowed to do their own work.

Boat yard boot camp was a good way to intimately get to know *Angel* and learn about her systems. I would be working on *Angel* full time for about three months and there was a lot to do. I had to replace her diesel, change out old hoses, through-hulls and those horrible gate style sea cocks, remove the old style head, replace *Angel's* rusty bobstay, and inspect other parts of her rigging.

These were just some of the significant jobs in store and I had a steep learning curve to tackle. Bill and I shared tools, an extension cord, and a leaky water hose. Being on the stands is a challenge for mariners who live aboard their vessels and can't afford staying in a hotel.

Unable to operate our boat's showers, we used the yard's rustic facilities, which were shared by wildlife and reclusive homeless people. The shower building was missing one of its doors and was open to the elements. Weeds grew in one of the shower stalls. At one point, a dog, or something large, had crapped in a stall. At least I hoped it was from a dog, because I kicked the offending turds out of the building in a fit of vexation.

Our sea legs rebelled against climbing the long, rickety ladders to our decks and some item would inevitably be forgotten, requiring more thigh burning trips. *Angel's* cabin became a jungle of tools, hoses, rags, dirty clothes, safety gear, and painting supplies. At night, raccoons rummaged through the garbage and scurried over our cabin tops. I knew this because of the tiny footprints left behind. Gangs of feral cats held midnight turf wars. Dawn's early light was accompanied by the crowing of roosters, until they were chased off by yipping dogs.

"Nice puppy," I said to a dog sniffing nearby. A fresh batch of epoxy was in a container near my feet. Oblivious to the yard office's "no unleashed pets" sign, the dog attempted his species' uncouth tactic of crotch sniffing. When I shied away, he casually lifted a leg and urinated on my epoxy. Bellowing, I threw a shoe. The rude dog yelped and scurried off.

Bill found this extremely funny and between bouts of laughter, he requested the hose. Frustrated by the day's direction, I plopped the hose in Bill's palm and an unintended burst of water sprayed his shirt.

"Hey! Why'd you squirt me for?" Bill said with a hurt expression.

"Sorry, it just went off," I explained, sincere. "The trigger's touchy, you have to—" Before I finished, Bill squirted himself in the head.

"Geez!" He blurted, "The handle sticks." He turned and when he tried to spray *Defiant*, no water came out. "Well ▓▓▓ me," Bill muttered, flinging the hose on the ground in disgust. It bounced on its handle and cold water geysered into Bill's forehead with enough force to push his hat backwards.

"▓▓▓▓▓▓" He kicked the hose and the water stopped. By now, I was the one who was laughing hysterically. Not amused, Bill stalked away, leaving a wet trail and a vociferous string of curse words only his Irish heritage could conjure up. His wet shoe prints went straight to the nearest pub. I followed.

Sitting at the tiny bar, we settled down with draft beers. A television caught Bill's eye. He was so focused on the flickering screen he didn't notice the bartender helpfully topping off his low beer level. Consequently, when Bill grabbed the mug, he poured the unexpected excess down his shirt. Indignant, he sputtered, cussed and slouched over the bar in dripping resignation.

"The universe just wants me to be wet," he announced woefully.

It was a relief to have a plan for *Angel's* failing diesel. I'd remove it, then clean and rebuild the engine bed to accommodate a larger model. R.C., a jovial diesel mechanic with a shaved head and hands like baseball mitts, and who'd once repaired fighter jets for a living, had a shop near the yard. Lucky for me, R.C. just happened to have a used, but functional, 20-horse Perkins for less than $2000. With his expert help and sizeable paws, this engine would soon be installed in *Angel*.

"Why have a motor?" A man with long hair asked, spitting out the last word with theatrical contempt. Preparing to change out *Angel's* old Cutless brand bearing before putting in the new-used diesel, I had removed the prop and was wet sanding crusty sea growth from her shaft. Polishing the rigid, silvery protrusion seemed strangely erotic. The man's query derailed my dirty train of thought.

"Wha–? Motor?" I said distractedly.

The man snorted and asked, "That your boat, aint it? Why waste time with motors?"

I rubbed my forehead, smearing it with grit. "Because *Angel* was born that way," I said, piqued by his slanderous stance. The man sniffed and regaled me with a wild tale of world circumnavigation in an engineless boat. After leading me along, he admitted that he'd just begun his trip. He had left the Keys and then returned after one day, apparently due to poor weather and not having enough supplies.

The act of boating is the same whether it's a brief cruise or a long-term, globe spanning trek. The same skills are utilized regardless. However, this guy was one of those pretentious, braggy types who implied that his planned circumnavigation somehow held more prestige than any other boating endeavor.

"You don't need motors," he concluded. "They take less skill."

He hastily left without answering my questions. I'd tried to ask if he had any experience using engines and why he hated them so much. Biased the other way, I loved powerboats and enjoyed rebuilding and repairing their engines. To me, possessing a combination of sails and an engine seemed like the best of both worlds.

An alternative source of propulsion was just another helpful tool for getting the most out of a trip on the water.

Angel's movements weren't limited by the vagaries of the wind and current. The man's erroneous belief that powered boats "take less skill" is ignorant. Even a child can quickly learn to sail a small, motor-free boat. Safely maneuvering a vessel under power and learning how to maintain her engine and its ancillary systems demands more experience and skill, not less.

Though, to see the man's point of view, I could understand how a person's sailing skills might atrophy if the sailboat's engine was relied on too frequently. Admittedly, it's too easy just to turn the key and effortlessly motor along. If the engine died, the sailboat owner should be capable of sailing out of trouble. It was basic common sense seamanship.

The next day, I installed *Angel's* new shaft bearing, hoping the anti-motor man wouldn't materialize and hiss in disapproval. Luckily for my diminishing sanity, he didn't. I respected, even appreciated, his opposing viewpoint, but didn't enjoy having it rammed in my face with such petulance.

A few other liveaboards shared the yard, working by day and staying in their boats at night. A few didn't work on their boats at all and others seemed to just be living there for the cheap rent. I minded my own business and stayed out of the way, but I couldn't help being creeped out by some of the boat yard denizens.

One troll like man would shut himself up all day in a rusted steel boat that was overgrown with weeds and had a gaping hole in one side. He never worked on it. The man only came out at night and would slink through the yard and into the dusty streets of Stock Island. Another fellow, one of the few who were actively working on their vessels, was always engaged in disagreements with a combative girlfriend.

to embrace the supernatural. She handed me a small, black box. "Rose deserves a better resting place than my closet."

I stared at the box of ashes in my hand, its contents once a living human being. I felt sad. The box was surprisingly heavy.

"Rose always loved the Caribbean and Bahamas," Stella said, her voice cracking. "Please take her with you." She hastily rubbed her eyes with a sleeve and looked away.

So *Angel* ended up with the solemn task of finding a final resting place for Rose. As our cruising season neared, Captain Bill and I prepared and provisioned. The box that was Rose was secured and placed in a safe spot near the chart table in *Angel*.

Because of the possibility that Rose had been haunting Stella's closet, I couldn't help but wonder about potential ghostly activity on my boat. Many of my relatives were highly superstitious and, when I was growing up, grandmother would freely speak of the presence of spirits. She would even helpfully point them out to us impressionable kids when she thought she was seeing one. We would be scared out of our wits. Bill tried to be just as helpful.

"*Angel's* going to be haunted!" Captain Bill announced over the VHF radio while we headed north, sailing along the Florida Bay side of the Keys. "What if it's bad luck? Maybe I'd better not sail too close to *Angel*, heh–heh, your ghost cooties will rub off on *Defiant*."

There were no unexplained bumps in the night, but we would face a season of highly active rain storm activity and, early in the trip, *Angel* began to suffer mechanical difficulties. Sailing when we could and then motoring through the tighter areas of the Florida Keys backcountry, we made it to Card Sound, a large and shallow bay behind north Key Largo. The winds had shifted and blew from the southwest, so Bill and I set our hooks in the lee off of Card Point. On the way there, we'd just been doused in a brief, but frighteningly robust and lightning loaded thunderstorm. It was a relief to be at rest for the night.

Earlier, when I was using *Angel's* diesel to motor through the backcountry's winding channels, it was running abnormally hot. Safe at anchor, I investigated the common culprits; raw water intake, internal coolant level, and raw water pump impeller. The pump's rubbery impeller had stiffened with age and was missing a blade, so I fished the broken piece out of the diesel's coolant tube stack and installed a new impeller. It was a time consuming, messy job requiring more rags and towels than I possessed.

Luckily, I always carried spares of engine parts that were utilized the most; gasket material, hose, impellers, crankcase oil, and transmission oil. I also kept spares such as injectors, glow plugs, and belts. Testing the simple repair, I ran the engine while at anchor and it seemed fine. Satisfied, smug even, I patted the box that was Rose and headed over to *Defiant* to share a couple of beers.

"You sure it wasn't your ghost giving you bad luck?" Bill asked, somewhat serious.

"I don't have a ghost," I responded, becoming peevish. "It's just a little box! It's not hurting anything. We're doing a good thing for Rose, finding her a nice resting spot. Sure better than a dark closet. So why would she haunt me?" I folded my arms, failing to conceal a growing uncertainty. "Right?"

"Uh-huh, okay. Whatever you say," Bill took a swig of beer, leaned back, and squinted at me. "I still think it is bad luck."

"You want to carry the box of dead body ashes for a while?"

"████ no!"

126

Sitting in *Defiant's* cockpit, we watched thunderstorms roll off the Everglades and flash over Florida's mainland to our north. The western sky grew luminous with streaks of orange and magenta as the sun set over the tattered remnants of rainclouds. Dropping the subject of ill luck or ghosts, Bill and I discussed tomorrow's goal of transiting through Biscayne Bay toward Miami. Our cell phones still working, Bill received a call from Bronwen, a friend and cruiser in southwest Florida. She was sailing her boat, *Sea Swan*, in our direction. She planned to meet us in Miami, and then cruise with us through the northernmost Bahamas.

As we retired to our respective boats, the southwest breeze, an unusual direction, became a gusty 15 to 20 knots, but the seas were smooth. I slept deeply until just after midnight. For seemingly no reason, I sat up in bed, suddenly wide awake. Vexed by the abrupt transition from rest to wakefulness, I rolled out of *Angel's* bunk. I peered outside. Peeling the bug screen from part of the companion way, I glanced around. In the light of a partial moon, I could see *Angel's* surroundings. Something was wrong.

Defiant was gone.

Hastily detangling from the bug screen, I jumped into the cockpit and fretfully scanned the dark waters. At first, I thought Bill had moved, but the idea made no sense. Then I spied what resembled *Defiant's* anchor light on the far end of Card Sound. Intuitively knowing it was my companion cruiser, I jumped into *Squishy* and raced toward the distant light. As I approached, the ketch could be seen, sideways to the wind. She was dragging anchor.

Pulling up to the boat's stern, I jump aboard, roused Bill, and blubbered at him. He woke in an instant. A shallow bank lay behind us and the drifting *Defiant* would soon run out of wiggle room.

"All right, calm down," Bill said, starting the engine. I assured *Squishy's* line wouldn't get into *Defiant's* propeller, and took the wheel while Bill pulled the anchor. He returned to the cockpit. I relinquished the helm.

"Wow, how did I get so far away?" Bill wondered out loud. "I must've been really sleeping!" Near *Angel* once again, *Defiant* set two hooks and tested them with his engine. Our boats remained in place, but neither of us slept as soundly for the night's remainder.

"*Angel's* running hot again," I radioed Bill when we used our engines to cross under Rickenbacker Causeway bridge on the way to Miami Marine Stadium.

"Maybe it's because the water temperature's so warm," Bill suggested. "Or your ghost is giving you bad luck."

"I don't have a ghost! But I do have to slow down, there's still something wrong with my diesel." Dismayed, I wondered what in the world the persistent problem could be. I gave Rose's box a sideways glance.

Anchored in the marine stadium, I attacked the diesel's problematic cooling system. The last thing to be checked, since it was so difficult to access, was the thermostat. If a thermostat failed to open sufficiently, an engine will overheat.

In an atypical location, my diesel's thermostat happened to be sandwiched behind the coolant water pump and between the exhaust manifold and the block. After making a significant mess, I pulled it out. Using the thermocouple that came with my multimeter to read the temperature, I suspended the thermostat in a pot of water and boiled it to see when it would open. It didn't open at all.

This had been the problem the whole time. I didn't have a spare thermostat, but using the diesel in tropical weather without one for a short while wasn't a big deal. The engine's reassembly was interrupted by an afternoon thunderstorm that spewed an ugly, black wall cloud over us.

The last thing *Angel* needed was to be threatened by a storm while she was partly disabled. I glanced at Rose's box and sighed.

Just before the storm's arrival, a family on a cruising sailboat had anchored a distance behind *Defiant* and parallel to a green sailboat. As the storm's powerful gust front hit, the green sailboat dragged anchor. The man on the family sailboat jumped into his inflatable and bounced over to render aid.

While he was doing this, his own boat blew sideways and started to drag away. A woman and a group of kids were standing in the boat's cockpit, watching their predicament and not doing a thing about it. One of the kids fell into the water with a great splash. The man raced back to his own boat to contend with the chaos. They eventually got settled, nobody was hurt, and the temporarily disabled *Angel* didn't drag.

"*Angel's* got a dead person onboard," Bill announced loudly, pointing at me. "She's haunted!"

"No she's not!" I shot Bill a look.

Bronwen and Bob slowly leaned forward, two sets of brows rising questioningly. Our friends had arrived to meet us in Miami. *Sea Swan* anchored near us and had promptly invited Bill and me over for an evening social.

A sail maker from South Africa, Bronwen enjoyed cruising and racing her 34-foot Morgan, a sailboat with classic lines that always turned heads. She was able to take some time off from her sail maker's business to join us. Always enjoying the company of her friends, an amiable gay gentleman named Bob had joined her for the adventure.

Informing them about *Angel's* unusual cargo, I explained how we'd set about honoring the special request of a good friend, Stella. I even told them about Stella's supposed closet haunting, with objects falling off the shelves and the door constantly creaking open. Bob and Bronwen were intrigued and enthusiastically volunteered to help us pick the right spot for Rose's ashes to rest. Now we weren't just cruising to play tourist, we had a meaningful mission.

"From what Stella's told and showed me with photos, Rose was a classy, gentle, grandmotherly old lady," I said, after reassuring them *Angel* was not haunted as Bill was claiming.

"And she grew marijuana," Bill said, straight-faced.

Hand over her mouth, Bronwen gasped, then grinned while Bob giggled. The idea of a weed purveying outlaw grandma, in life a matronly, plump, white haired elder, had its entertaining element.

After four days of waiting out unusually stormy weather, *Sea Swan*, *Defiant*, and *Angel* bee lined toward the Bahamas. A southerly 13 knot wind increased over the course of our Gulf Stream crossing. By day's end, a firm wind gusting to 20 knots blew toward the Little Bahama Bank. The sometimes strong counter current along West End made conditions rough with steep, irregular seas.

Angel, the smallest vessel in the group, struggled and lagged far behind. Standing, feet spread and wedged in the cockpit, I steered over the awkward seas, tiller pulling hard. *Angel* rose up and then roughly slid off each wave with a stomach lurching, rig-shaking clash. *Angel* only had the staysail out and it still seemed like too much sail area. I longingly eyed the thin, hazy strip of land ahead.

The winds continued to increase and conditions were too rough to safely slip into Indian Cay pass. Capt. Bill, the closest to land, could see the area with binoculars and was sure he could detect the foaming, white crests of breaking waves, possibly steep enough to roll a vessel sideways and broach her into the rocks. Discussing our situation over the VHF, *Sea Swan*, *Defiant*, and *Angel* bounced and slammed toward Memory Rock instead. The sun was beginning to set and we were running out of visibility.

When we were halfway between Memory Rock and Indian Cay, the water was deep enough to cross onto the bank. The rocky barrier to the bank had been replaced by sand. Salty, tired, and sore, our caravan fled from the Atlantic's edge. Reveling in the smoother seas, we continued toward Mangrove Cay. We anchored there, picked up our jumbled messes on our cabin floors, and crashed into our respective bunks.

The days alternated between rain and fair, our three vessels making their way to Green Turtle Cay. We'd arrived in the out islands just in time for Regatta Time in Abaco, that party-like series of sailboat races. Rose remained on *Angel* while we were suddenly swept into the action.

Sea Swan had signed up to race in the cruiser's class and Bill crewed for Bronwen while I alternated between helping *Sea Swan* and our Bahamian friends on *Abaco Rage*. The well organized annual regatta was an opportunity to socialize with the locals and enjoy some friendly competition with other cruisers who normally don't race. Many entries were strictly cruising boats, some with entire families onboard and dinghies swaying in their davits.

Many participating vessels would try to come every year. Carl and Suzi on *Glory Daze* were familiar faces, and I was thrilled to see them again. During at least one year of
a painted smiley face underwater

New Zealanders Dave and Chrissy were back on *Keweloa* and had entered their vessel into the races. *Keweloa's* sails, which sported a stylish image of three dolphins, were frequently photographed by tourists in rented powerboats. Unfortunately, one of those curious boats had swung by too closely and ran over the fishing line Dave was trailing. Dave's fishing rod was broken in half and this time he got █████ in the American way.

Not to miss the fun, my sister, Krista, flew down to visit and crew on *Sea Swan*. While I grew up as the pragmatic and introverted geekish sibling, Krista was the one endowed with good looks and a vivacious, extroverted personality. As a youth, she'd be sneaking off to party with her friends. They'd engage in rambunctious kid things; visiting video arcades, playing pranks on people, and stealing into adult flicks at the movie theater. I'd be in my room and lost in books or experimenting with electric motors and miniature solar panels.

Krista was an instant hit at the sailor's parties, a cloud of men orbiting around her where ever she went. During the second day of racing, Krista formulated some of her own race tactics.

"That cruiser's getting closer," Bill said, peering around *Sea Swan's* full headsail. The day's race was intense and vessels were close. "We've gotta block their wind."

"Okay, I see it," Bronwen said as she helmed her boat.

"The main sail's getting slack," Bob observed. Krista jumped into action and helped, her and Bob tailing and cranking

"I just knew it. I could feel that she was finally at peace." Stella said. "And my closet stopped making noise."

27

Southeast Florida's ICW

After crossing back to Florida together, we enjoyed one last cockpit social with Bob and Bronwen before they had to sail onward and return to their work schedules. Bill and I remained in Lake Worth for a day before planning our route to the Florida Keys. Since the weather was too unstable to safely proceed on the Atlantic side, *Defiant* and *Angel* took the inside route and lived to tell about it. The inside route is part of southeast Florida's Intracoastal Waterway, also known as the ICW. The ICW runs the length of the entire east coast and is a travel way for private and commercial vessels.

"Live Bait," read a sign on a boat anchored beyond the buoys. The water was rippling with boat wakes, and two recreational fishermen pulled up to the floating vendor. In the faint light of dawn, Lake Worth was wide awake. *Angel* wasn't. My Bayfield cutter reluctantly submitted to her diesel as it dragged her into the channel. Bill was much more alert. He was eager for a chance to take the scenic route and travel through the ICW. I wasn't thrilled about the idea of having to motor all day. I didn't enjoy the ICW in the past and assumed that it would be the same tedium this time around.

"Don't chicken out now," Bill radioed after I admitted my reservations. Partial to open seas and claustrophobic in the cluttered crush of urban areas, I preferred the Atlantic. Southeastern Florida's ICW route was interestingly scenic, and I was glad that I didn't "chicken out" after all.

Ahead lay one of the busiest, most populated stretches of the Intracoastal Waterway on the lower east coast. From St. Lucie to South Miami, the waterway runs through a megalopolis and narrows to canal like proportions in many places. The route is densely encased in tall buildings and mansions.

Restricted schedule bridges are abundant. *Angel* and *Defiant* would have to open 36 bridges in only 50 nautical miles. Here, boaters see the largest cruise ship ports in the world, and Fort Lauderdale boasts the highest number of vessels in the state. Military ships with security zones, tugs and barges, and container ships frequent the larger inlets.

The advantage is that southbound cruisers don't have to fight the Gulf Stream, which sweeps close to shore here. Boats also find relief from inclement weather and rough seas. Sailboats with drafts of seven feet or less and masts 55 feet and under can comfortably travel through this part of the ICW. Most east coast fixed bridges have a 65 foot clearance.

Traveling is usually easier during the weekdays, when south Florida tends to be less chaotic. Off season, from early summer to late fall, is also a less crowded time.

The procedure to open a bridge is like elsewhere, but Florida tenders use VHF channel 09 instead of the usual channel 13. When approaching and the bridge is in sight, a boat hails the bridge by its name, identifies vessel type; sailboat or powerboat, vessel's name, and direction of travel. The bridge usually radios back, providing its next opening time or if it'll open on demand. It's wise to acknowledge that you received the information and are standing by on channel 09. Bridge schedules are always changing, so communicating by radio also allows you to know exact opening times, facilitating cruising plans.

A cruising guide or charts listing bridge names is necessary so one can radio the correct bridge without confusion. At one point, I misread the guidebook and used the wrong name when hailing the next bridge. Two bridges had responded. The tenders see plenty of puzzled new visitors, and the correct bridge that saw *Angel's* approach helpfully set me back on track.

Water currents average 1 to 1 ½ knots in most areas. Confusingly, current direction always seemed to vary from inlet to inlet. The waters around Hillsboro Inlet and Bakers Haulover Inlet had the strongest currents, and at one point, *Angel* was slowed to 3.8 knots, my rotund boat frantically waddling against the flow at full throttle.

The lake-like area at Bakers Haulover Inlet is prone to sandy shoaling, and boats must stay in the channel. Yellow tags at the top end demarcate all ICW markers, helping to prevent boats from straying off course due to numerous non-ICW markers leading to inland rivers or canals.

The need to constantly tend the helm makes it difficult for singlehanders when we need to use the head or grab a snack. For obvious reasons, using an autopilot isn't feasible in this part of the ICW. Planning shorter days, stopping at boat-in restaurants or marinas, or throwing a lunch hook in a pocket of water out of harm's way are always options.

"*Angel* cleared, thank you for the opening, Lake Avenue," I radioed after passing through Lake Avenue Bridge's span and gawking at the massive gears and machinery within its works. Likewise, *Defiant* let the tender know when he was through. With their double duty responsibilities of watching heavy road and water traffic, bridge tenders appreciate common courtesy and clear communication. When treated with honest courtesy, some were quite mirthful, wishing us a good day or waving at us from their windowed, bird's eye view.

Continuing south, after Boynton Inlet, the ICW narrows again and is framed by concrete. After seeing an anchored sailboat with her bowsprit unnaturally bent skyward from some traumatic impact, my claustrophobic feelings returned. Farther south, Delray Beach offered numerous marinas with transient spaces and boat in restaurants. The next two cities, Boca Raton and Pompano Beach, also provide vibrant cultural scenes.

"...kick those squirrels in the butt and follow me," the tug's captain suggested. Pushing a construction barge, *Mark* the tug was just ahead of us. Squirrels appropriately kicked, *Angel* and *Defiant* settled behind our friendly escort. Tugs with barges and emergency vessels can open restricted-schedule bridges at any time. If you travel behind a tug, you still must radio the bridge tenders to inform them of your intentions, and they'll let you pass through behind the tug.

Later, when *Mark* cautioned us that he planned to make a starboard turn, we acknowledged and kept clear. These fellow mariners work hard all day, and we were on vacation, so the least we could do was not be in their way or make a nuisance of ourselves. The tug reached its destination, and we were alone again. By now, those claustrophobic concerns had eased, and my tight, sweaty grip on the tiller relaxed.

We were soon motoring through Fort Lauderdale. A confusing maze of canals branched from the ICW here, and traffic was thick even on an off season weekday. To secure space at a local marina, advanced reservations are recommended. Too tired to hunt down marina slips, *Angel* and *Defiant* anchored in Lake Sylvia, just north of Port Everglades. Deep all around, the tiny lake was dredged. This place was for brief respites only. Lake Sylvia is bordered by buildings, daytime traffic is frequent, and I was uncertain about holding in its soft mud bottom.

"They're swarming me," *Defiant* radioed. A flock of small, excitable sailboats, herded by two inflatables, commandeered the lake's corner. It was a local youth sailing group. Fun to watch, the giggling kids sparred in races and repeatedly dunked themselves in capsize drills. They seemed to enjoy the dunking part. To Bill's chagrin, and my amusement, they were using *Defiant* as an unofficial racing mark.

By early evening, it quieted down. The annoying wakes of local boats pulling kids on inner tubes, and everything else towable, ceased and the city's nightscape blazed with incandescent color. The top of one building was illuminated in such a way that it resembled a stereotypical flying saucer.

Fort Lauderdale soon blended into Hollywood. A cruising friend was in the area, and we convened at the canal-front restaurant, Le Tub. *Angel* tied to Le Tub's sea wall, a courtesy for boater patrons. The branches of tall trees hung over the dock. *Angel's* rigging swept against the foliage as she pulled up. An abundance of twigs, leaves, and seeds rained onto my deck and over the dock.

Patrons at Le Tub's waterfront tables stopped what they were doing and stared. A boy was fishing along the shore on the opposing side of the canal. Even he stopped casting to watch. *Angel* and I felt like the self-conscious stranger entering an old western saloon where the animated chatter and music suddenly ceases as all heads turn and stare.

Defiant anchored nearby in the six-foot deep mouth of the tiny North Lake. North Lake's water was an opaque dark brown, its unseen bottom mushy. A small yacht club was located along one side of this tiny lake. I felt safe enough secured to the eatery. Open daily from noon to 4:00 in the morning, Le Tub is a social oasis with dense greenery in lieu of walls. Found nautical objects served as décor, along with painted porcelain toilet bowls as whimsical planters.

The hand written menu offered a simple, reasonably priced selection. Adjacent to Le Tub was a pizza place, liquor store, Greek restaurant, bakery, and a food mart. These places were all accessible by boat. Just across the street was public beach access. Enjoying our friend's company and Le Tub's rustic bar, we stayed the night.

Next morning, we planned to spend the day shopping in town. I released *Angel* from the dock and motored over to *Defiant* to drop anchor near Bill. A police boat idled up to me.

"Is he with you?" The stern officer gruffly queried, gesturing at the anchored *Defiant*.

"Uh, yeah," I said, distracted, in the middle of contending with *Angel's* muddy ground tackle and pinching my fingers from the distraction. We hadn't done anything wrong, so I assumed I'd been targeted for a vessel safety check. The frowning cop asked how long we were staying and eagerly wanted to know if we would leave. He stared at me with what only could be described as distain.

"So you're hauling anchor and leaving today then–" he urged, idling away. It was more of a demand than a query.

The officer's subtly antagonistic approach clearly indicated we weren't welcome. Our vessels were silent, ship-shape and unobtrusive, and we were spending money ashore, so the offensive reception was puzzling. It's not as if we were getting naked, blasting music, or behaving like drunks and shouting at passerby. Our boats were out of anyone's way.

After pounding through storms and navigating to remote islands for hundreds of miles, we were in no mood to be treated with such unmerited crassness. Disgusted, we shopped elsewhere and hastily left the next morning.

When I visit the same area via rent-a-car, the city is always welcoming. No one in their right mind would pull up and demand that I hurry up and leave. Apparently no longer viewed as valid tourists because of our transportation choice, we weren't good enough for Hollywood, Florida.

Stretching southward, we motored past the impressively tall buildings of Miami. Heading into the Miami Marine stadium, *Defiant* and *Angel* stopped there to rest. When I attempted to take *Squishy* into the nearby Rickenbacker Marina, so I could learn more about their services and shop at the ship's store, I experienced yet another pointless encounter from the hate-first-ask-questions-later antagonistic type.

A Rickenbacker Marina staff member who'd watched me pulling up to what was obviously a small vessel dock, turned to face me, folded his arms, and glared. The effect was oddly immature. Before I could ask about transient slips, or anything, he raised his voice, vigorously flapped an arm at me and shouted something about "private" and that I had to go away.

Recalling our coarse treatment in Hollywood, I shook my head in disgust and motored back to *Angel*. The cruising guide didn't indicate that Rickenbacker Marina was private and not just closed to traveling sailboats, but outright hostile toward them. I had the impression that if I'd arrived by car to patronize their ship's store, my greeting would've been less malicious.

It's a bizarre and senseless human foible to condemn someone based on their conveyance. I'm the same person with the same stupid, fly-away wallet, yet in Florida one's reception radically differs according to the mode of transportation one arrives in. This was getting annoying.

With a completely opposite reception, Crandon Park Marina welcomed our patronage instead. This friendly boater's stop is located just south of the Rickenbacker Causeway and perfectly sheltered in a cove on Key Biscayne. Crandon Park actually treated us like human beings and the staff went out of their way to be helpful. *Defiant* pulled up to the fuel dock to fill up on diesel. There are both transient slips and moorings, but the marina happened to be full when we arrived. With its professionalism and reasonable attitude, we weren't surprised.

28

When Squirrels Attack

Passing south through Miami's last bridge, the fixed Rickenbacker Causeway, is always a relief for me. The concrete confines of the city finally give way to the open, attractive waters of Biscayne Bay. With just a short turn to our right, we stopped at Dinner Key. At the time, the marina there had a private mooring area, so we anchored outside.

This area is exposed to the east and only comfortable in calmer weather. Skittish from our recent treatment, we were relieved when we faced no pointless hostility and encountered cheerful people. Dinner Key was an interesting stop and a good place to obtain provisions. There's a convenient bus stop for travel into Miami.

Allowed to use a dinghy dock at Dinner Key, we went ashore and tentatively explored, still wary of being confronted by some antagonistic, hateful official. We were amazed when this did not happen, but we did experience a confrontation of the wild kind.

After lunch, Bill and I walked across a parking lot near Coconut Grove. I was carrying a box containing extra food and mindlessly picking out of it. In an open area of the parking lot, a squirrel bounded toward me in that fuzzy, fluid motion they always seemed to have.

I chuckled and pointed as the squirrel stopped just a few feet away. With intense interest, he watched me eat. Unable to resist, I tossed him a crumb. Suddenly, more squirrels arrived, seeking the same treatment.

"Here," I said to Bill, "Check this out. I used to have little guys like these in my yard when I had a house." Sitting down, I moved slowly, setting food near my leg and watching the brazen squirrels reach for the treats.

Unfortunately, the twitchy city critters were less timid than their rural cousins. They jumped on my legs, lap, and one leapt on my back and then kicked off with prickly claws. I made a brief squealing noise. Without help from me, they scrabbled at the box of food, acting as if they hadn't eaten in months. Attracted by their frenzied pals, downy tails twitching, more fluffy miscreants dashed toward me.

"Don't move!" Bill said, backing away. "Er...uh, cover your eyes or something." Looking doubtful, he stepped behind a parked car.

"Awwwk!" I said, tossing the food box aside. The squirrels pounced at it in a rippling, furry wave. Scrambling to my feet, I dashed toward Bill, who was laughing now. "Gee, some help you are." I shoved him sideways. That only made him laugh harder.

29

Key Largo to the Lower Keys

The ship's clock read 2:00am. I'd just been jolted out of bed by a frightful hissing and squealing noise. Growing louder, the steady sound reverberated throughout *Angel's* hull. I scurried outside. The dark sea was placid. Then, a great mass of objects thudded against *Angel's* bottom while the water erupted in a thrashing froth. Two large shapes surfaced behind me with snorkeler-like exhalations of air. Dolphin!

Using echolocation and creating what seemed to be a fizzing net of bubbles, hungry bottlenose dolphin were corralling schools of fish, headfirst, against *Angel's* nether parts. The stunned fish were easy prey. For the rest of the night, my innocent sailboat was the centerpiece for a rowdy, all-you-can-eat seafood buffet.

"I slept so good last night," Bill said after I paddled over to his boat for a social breakfast. "We anchored in a great spot."

146

I blearily eyed him over my coffee and grunted in response. At least somebody had a restful night. We were anchored in a seven foot deep pocket near the inlet to Key Largo Harbor Marina on the Atlantic side. A few miles to our south lay the uninhabited Rodriguez Key, an anchoring stop for travelers. It offers soft bottom holding and protection from most compass points except due east, since its west side is an ankle deep tidal flat.

Squishy's outboard reattached, I collected Bill and we nosed into the channel. It was framed by ostentatious houses and I feared that we were lost. However, Key Largo Harbor Marina was found near the canal's 90-degree turn. Gas, diesel, and water are available until closing time at 5:00pm.

Proceeding down the canal, one will find Marina Del Mar and Holiday Inn with slips close to groceries and a shopping center. Restaurants along the seawall, like Sharkeys Pub and Galley, and Coconuts, offer dinghy dockage for patrons. Tying *Squishy* out of the way, we investigated Sharkeys, which is adjacent to a shop called Ocean Divers.

The subtropical Keys comprise North America's only living coral barrier reef and it encompasses about 2,800 square nautical miles. Not to be outdone, Florida Bay boasts the world's largest sea grass bed. Surrounded by both, it's only natural that Key Largo's claim to fame is its aquatic scene. John Pennekamp State Park is 178 square nautical miles of submerged splendor with historic shipwrecks, coral reef jungles, and a famous underwater statue known as Christ of the Abyss.

With a mask, snorkel and fins, you can pay a visit to a bubbly fairyland bejeweled with tropical fish and shimmering corals. Dive gear will take you deeper into the muted blues of mysterious places populated by bug eyed sea creatures. Silent and spooky, they peer at you from the eerie graveyards of sunken ships.

You'll never know what you'll see since over five thousand different species of marine life comprise the reef and sea grass bed ecosystems. We snorkeled by using the free public mooring buoys that are found at dive sites along Hawk Channel. Sheltered mooring buoys inside Largo Sound were also available for a fee.

After a day experiencing Key Largo, we rafted up since the weather was so calm. *Defiant* hung on her own hook while I approached with *Angel*. Bill reached for my lines and helped me settle in. Masts and rigging were spaced to avoid snags should a large wake rock us. If the weather changed, *Angel* could motor clear in a matter of minutes. Under an electric Key Largo sunset, we lounged in our cockpits and watched the world go by. A family idled past in a pontoon boat and a little girl's voice was overheard.

"Oh look!" She said, pointing at us. "A mommy and daddy sailboat! Will they have a baby?" Looking embarrassed, a woman hushed the imaginative child while they idled onwards. Amused, I chuckled. Bill rolled his eyes.

"Just to clarify things," he said. "*Angel* is, without a doubt, the girl boat."

As Bill and I wound our way through the emerald luster of the middle Keys, the island chain worked its seductive magic. Sunsets are vivid and the mostly clear waters inspire the soul. Traveling on the Atlantic side, we made way for Moser Channel, which passes under the fixed 65-foot Seven Mile Bridge. It's just west of the city of Marathon on Vaca Key.

Stopping for the night, *Angel* and *Defiant* anchored bayside. We were close enough to take a dinghy into Boot Key Harbor for supplies. The aged bascule bridge that used to pivot up for boats entering Boot Key is now permanently open.

The city's dinghy dock is on the harbor's northern side, midway. A hardware store is within walking distance several blocks east along HWY 1. Dinghy dock prices for transients have bounced around over the years, and were absurdly expensive. By the year 2014, the dingy dock fee was a whopping $22 dollars a day. Boot Key's protected waters are overrun by city moorings, and there were pricey moorings for transients. I couldn't help but wonder if the excessive fees were designed to welcome only the wealthy, who could afford the access, while discriminating against the working class.

Fueling was easy at Burdines Waterfront, which is located along the entrance into Boot Key harbor before reaching the open bascule bridge. Bill noticed a cooler full of beer on the dock, but he was unwilling to disturb the slumbering marina cat sprawled on the cooler's lid. Bill stood over the big, orange cat and drooled until another thirsty boater came to the rescue. Above the marina is a restaurant that locals refer to as Burdines and tourists may know it as the Chiki Tiki Bar and Grille.

After an overnight rest at anchor, *Angel* and *Defiant* continued along the lower Florida Keys. This world of water, sun, coconut palms, and the rum based mojito made us forget what day it was. And we didn't care. Small town charm greeted us at Big Pine Key, home of the National Key Deer Wildlife Refuge. Offshore, the Looe Key reef treats snorkelers and divers to a wealth of marine splendor.

The nearby Bahia Honda State Park, offers a white sand beach that's been rated the second most beautiful in the nation. Boaters can anchor nearby and explore the park's nature trails. In Hawk channel, we sailed toward Key West. This island port is the last piece of civilization before jumping to the uninhabited Marquesas and the Dry Tortugas, located west of Key West.

30

Key Weird

Near Key West's busy harbor, a strong current and a fading breeze was on the nose, so I started *Angel's* diesel. Responding to one of those unexplainable intuitive pulls, I peeked behind the engine cover and noticed a slow ooze of seawater beyond the seal on the raw water pump. Not a serious problem, yet, *Angel* could still motor along and seek an anchoring spot.

As always, Key West harbor was buzzing with boats of all kinds. A historic wooden schooner named *Western Union*, deep sea fishermen, kayaks, parasail tour boats, and a large Coast Guard cutter composed the moment's activity.

Bill took *Defiant* past Mallory Dock, where the daily Sunset Celebration had been a local ritual for at least a few decades. Two massive cruise ships, the tallest things around, blocked Malloy Dock. Deeper in the harbor, I noticed a collection of surveillance cameras and a rotating radar unit that were trained on the water and anchorages. Innocent citizens are now being spied on offshore as much as we are watched ashore. In a fleeting moment of rebellious impudence, I struggled to refrain from making a face, or worse, at the nearest camera.

Arriving boats can check into one of Key West's marinas or pay for a mooring on Fleming Key's east side. Boats also attempt to anchor on Fleming Key's west side or around the uninhabited Wisteria Island, but care must be taken when maneuvering around the derelict boats. These immobile, degenerating hulks are sometimes occupied. Some of those occupants possess questionable mental stability. Most of the vessels anchored around the area are transient visitors or honest, working class boating enthusiasts who simply can't afford the unrealistic cost of Key West housing.

To anchor, a good set is needed for the silt and grass bottom, which is the consistency of pudding in most parts of the anchoring areas. *Angel* drug in 20 knot winds the first time she attempted to grab a hold of the seafloor with a single anchor and chain. Two anchors in tandem on a single rode is an old trick that has not failed me here, excluding freak storms, and is worth the hassle of assembly.

Since about the mid 2000s, Key West city officials began cultivating the island's reputation for open hostility against individuals who choose to live aboard boats. I've seen and heard liveaboards libeled in local newspapers, and slandered on local radio and cable TV programs.

As with Marathon and Boot Key, Key West has also gained a reputation for constant marine police harassment and stalking, late night raids of people's boats, and unconstitutional sweeps. On the positive side, most local businesses do not extend such enmity and welcome the traveling mariner. Many establishments go out of their way to help cruisers who are new to this area.

Mindful of Key West's bipolar attitude, I installed 12-volt, onboard hidden security cameras that can easily be triggered by me or by intruders. Should I be brutalized by some gung-ho, sociopathic law officer, the hidden cameras would capture every word and visual detail as it was streamed live to the internet.

After minor repairs to our boats, Bill and I played tourist. For a fee, there's a dinghy dock in front of Turtle Kraals restaurant. Lock the dinghy and motor, and hide anything of value. The Historic Seaport and boardwalk is a must see, but it's easy to get waylaid by the attractive restaurants and shops along the route.

Bill and I were drawn to the Key West Bait and Tackle Shop across from Turtle Kraals. Not only did this charming, family-owned store offer fishing gear and outdoor goods, but they had a small bar with cold drinks, personable bartenders, and just as personable regulars.

A few blocks west is Old Town's Duval Street and its party zone of shops, pubs, cafes, and galleries. A diversity of downtown museums, I counted thirteen at the time, educate and entertain. Fantasy Fest, Hemingway days, Goombay, art fairs, live theatre, music festivals, and historic re-creations are just some of the popular events. The locals here are phenomenal; their creativity, dedication, and diversity giving Key West its true charm.

Within walking distance from the downtown seaport, there's coin laundry, a library, a small and overpriced grocer, the knowledgeable staff at Key West Marine Hardware, Ace Hardware, and a West Marine. For groceries, it's best to go uptown. The family owned Key West Marine Hardware carries a selection of hard to find goods and they'll usually order an item if it's not in stock.

A well established local and tourist hangout is the waterfront Schooner Wharf Bar and Grill. This open air establishment still retains the old flavor of Key West and it is extremely active in the community. Owners Paul and Evalena Worthington are sailors and had built their now popular business out of the cockpit of a wooden schooner. The bar itself is constructed of old shrimp boat and schooner parts.

"That construction worker leered at me," I complained to Bill as we walked along the Key West's ever busy Roosevelt Boulevard.

"What's new about that?" He said, shrugging.

"But – but – it was a woman!" I said, flattered.

"What's new about that?" Bill repeated, smirking, "It's Key West."

A day later, we met our friend Stella and she invited us to a party. The social gathering was a late November Thanksgiving Day picnic that Stella had helped organize. It was intended for people who were away from their families for the holidays. Highly active in her community, the remarkable Stella has been involved in things like marine construction and salvage, and has lived in exotic, far away locales. When she talked, we listened. Her sense of humor would always inspire us.

"I made the mistake of falling asleep on the bench in the aviary," Stella was saying after we asked about the time she'd raised tame birds. "When I woke up a few hours later, the birds had been roosting on me. I was covered in poop!"

When Thanksgiving Day arrived, Bill and I walked, cradling offerings of beer, into the party we'd been invited to. Seated at rough, wooden picnic tables in the sunny outdoors, we had dinner with an odd group that included a manic depressive, an amputee, heavily tattooed bikers, and a menagerie of loudly honking ibis. Lurking nearby were two cats and a semi-tame raccoon.

Feeling awkward and out of place, Bill and I ended up absently drinking most of the beer we'd brought. We searched for Stella, but our selflessly busy friend had already scurried off to volunteer at a nearby church.

Unable to consume ham or poultry, but not wishing to offend our elderly hosts, I secretly started giving the animals my food. Big mistake. The wildlife quickly surrounded the picnic tables, ibis greedily rustling around our ankles. One of the cats hissed and jumped on the platter of ham. The fearless raccoon dashed under the table, scattering the ibis in a honking, wing flapping squabble. Some of the startled diners jumped back and others made plaintive squeaking noises. The largest biker of the bunch blustered and shouted at the cat.

"Look what you did, bubblehead!" Bill said while facing forward and whispering from the side of his mouth, which had food in it. He finished chewing. "Uh, that raccoon's staring at you."

"I, er– " The raccoon under the table grabbed the remaining turkey out of my limp hand.

"Shhh! Anybody asks, we don't know nothing." He produced a toothpick and proceeded to use it. "Are you going to drink that last beer?"

"I, um…"

"That's okay, I'll finish it." He removed the beer's cap and took a generous swig. Leaning back, he stifled a belch.

By afternoon's end, the manic depressive was weeping, the grumpy elderly folk were arguing, and the turkey eating raccoon was trying to wrap its greasy, clammy paws around my finger. Oh, and I needed more beer. The bikers had already roared away on their Harleys.

"Only in Key West," Bill said with a grin as we hastily departed for the comfort of our boats.

31

The Gifts of December

In Key West, Sargasso's mooring was checked, and the dinghy loaded with luggage. Enjoying their early start, Jacqui and Steve McCann motored to shore. They drove to the mainland where a family holiday gathering awaited. Canadians Steve and Jacqui have ventured all over the world, traveling in everything from canoes to cruise ships.

Interested in exploring on their own schedule and desiring more comfort than camping or canoes, they'd recently purchased a used sailboat named *Sargasso*. Steve and Jacqui took sailing lessons and had plenty of practice, but it wasn't easy.

Peevish, *Sargasso* liked to drag anchor, and her boom would fall off at odd times. Falling into the water between sailboat and dinghy happened more often than the couple liked. The technically minded Jacqui spent lots of time righting old wrongs in the engine room, and Steve's wallet was hijacked by the boat's neediness. However, the holidays were here. It was time to take a break and get festive.

Later, on the other side of the island where *Sargasso* was moored, two restless travelers stirred in the vaporous light of dawn. *Defiant* and *Angel* raised sail and rode a faint breeze toward the Gulf of Mexico. As the rising sun floated overhead, the wind faded.

A cool mist thickened, lacing its damp tendrils around us. The sea was a grey mirror. No other vessels were out, and the silence was unsettling. Bill and I didn't have a plan, but had simply sailed into the Gulf and toward the backcountry of the lower Keys. We had a few days off of work and wanted to enjoy it by sailing.

"Where is everybody?" I radioed.

"Duh! It's Christmas morning," Bill responded. "People are home, opening gifts and stuff." Sails tucked back in, *Defiant* proceeded under power and I followed. Bill didn't observe any holiday customs. More interested in the spiritual beliefs of my native ancestors, I didn't participate in mainstream religious beliefs or traditions either.

Unfortunately, my family's traditional ways had been scattered to the winds. The elders were gone and today's pop culture was the norm. I wondered why I still clung to a thread that no longer seemed connected. I didn't feel like I culturally belonged to anything. It was a lost and lonely feeling to not completely know the old traditions. Moping, I motored along in silence, not noticing the growing fog.

"This weather's weird," *Defiant* radioed. "Visibility's getting bad and my engine's acting a little weird." Before I could respond, a small shape emerged from the mist and swept toward *Angel*. The apparition landed on the port spreader. Claws clinking on metal. A hawk! Returning my startled stare, the bird fluffed its feathers and settled in.

After an hour of calm motoring, the hawk remained in *Angel's* rigging, watching me with fiery eyes. A revered symbol in native tradition, the hawk is considered to be a spiritual messenger. The bird flew in from the west, a direction where the souls of the ancestors are believed to reside.

I rubbed my eyes, unable to stifle the flow of tears. I had the distinct impression that the old ways were not lost but safe within. The thread was still connected. The elders still spoke. After some time, the bird took flight and vanished in the fog. Awed, *Defiant* and *Angel* motored onward.

Tired after a sociable Christmas day, Steve and Jacqui drove back to Key West. It was late and they looked forward to a good night's sleep on Sargasso. At the dark dinghy dock, Steve started the outboard and warmed it up. Satisfied all was well, he shut it off and the pair loaded the dinghy with gear, luggage, and extra groceries.

When Steve tried to restart the motor, nothing happened. Panicky, he kept trying while Jacqui stood on the dock and encouraged him. Misjudging the dock's width in the dark, she took a step backward and fell in the water. Steve helped her, cold and salty, into the dinghy and the two resolved to paddle to *Sargasso*. It was windy, choppy and no other boats were out.

"What else could possibly go wrong?" Steve exclaimed, just after his paddle broke. "I don't believe this!" The overloaded dinghy limped back to shore. Jacqui showered at the nearby marina facilities and, joined by another stranded boater, a midnight dinner was shared by the light of a camp stove. Unable to return to their vessels, they slept in their cars. The next morning, Steve's unpredictable outboard started and the couple finally made it to *Sargasso*.

Plagued by engine trouble, fog, and an unexpected squall, *Defiant* and *Angel* fled back to Key West. *Defiant's* electric fuel pump was failing and *Angel's* diesel was being plagued by an air leak. At least the squall had roused some wind so we could sail and only use our compromised engines when we really needed them. Bill and I managed to safely anchor.

Disappointed, we took *Squishy* toward shore and spied a boat named *Sargasso* tied to the docks. She was a 36-foot Morgan Out Island, built the same year as *Defiant*. Intrigued, we stopped by and met Steve and Jacqui.

They relayed their Christmas night dinghy adventure and told us about an earlier anchor dragging scare where tackle was lost and deck hardware ruined. Because of that, they'd moved into the city mooring field, but *Sargasso* broke from her mooring.

Naturally, all these things had to happen at night in bad weather. Steve admitted he was ready to give up the cruising idea. Everything just seemed to break or go wrong. Our failed travel plans forgotten, Bill and I encouraged the couple not to give up. We shared some of our own too numerous cruising misadventures.

"You mean other people make these mistakes, too?" Steve questioned. "It's not just us?"

We assured the pair they weren't alone. The boater's learning process takes time. Lots of it. Encouraged, Steve and Jacqui agreed to follow us on an overnight caravan sail to a nearby island, after we addressed our engine problems. When we embarked on our social sail, Bill and I got to know this delightful couple from Canada.

"You really don't do anything for Christmas?" Steve asked, looking surprised. "It's too commercial," Bill explained, shrugging. "People get crazy and stressed, and while I try to respect people's religions, I don't like their beliefs being pushed on me."

Waving his hand, Steve impressed us with his view of Christmas. It's not the consumerism, taking things in a stressful way or religious pushiness. It's about people. It's about joy and meaningful connection with others. And who could resist the magic of glittering holiday decor to brighten a grey winter's day? A writer and musician, Steve gave us a gift, a CD with an elegant song he'd recorded called *The Meaning of Christmas*.

Those past few days, I learned some new ways of observing things. Under the wide diversity of traditions, customs, and beliefs, it truly is about people. Whatever beliefs we're raised with, we're all connected. We do belong. Mankind, who foolishly tends to focus on perceived differences instead similarities, who likes to divide, categorize, and label, is in reality part of the same whole.

Like that hawk, we just have to rise above the ground's limits and see the greater picture. Memorable gifts were given this season. A rare bird delivered a spiritual message. A couple new to cruising got the encouragement they needed. Bill and I received a happier perspective on the real meaning of the holidays.

The next few months passed by quickly and before we knew it, spring arrived with firm sailing winds. Bill and I took a few days off for a boating excursion to an intriguing ring of small islands west of Key West.

32

The Mysterious Marquesas

At first glance, the flat cluster of mangrove isles didn't look like much.

"Another mosquito feeding station," Bill commented while slapping and then scratching his leg. As if we'd just landed on another world, the two of us waded toward shore, the only human presence around. We had taken Bill's skiff to tour inside the Marquesas. It wasn't long before we found ourselves completely enchanted by the remote, atoll like ring of islands. We'd ventured into a place of mystery, rich with treasure hunter's legends, pirate lore, and a precious and delicate ecosystem.

About four miles in diameter, the Marquesas are about 17 nautical miles west of Key West. It's part of a national wildlife refuge and there are some rules. No overnight camping is allowed onshore, and the bugs make such an endeavor a poor idea anyways. There are 300-foot no motor zones around the three smallest islets on the west side.

However, boats can anchor overnight inside the lagoon-like Mooney Harbor, or anywhere on the outside of the island ring.

Boaters new to the area benefit by doing what we did, entering Mooney Harbor by dinghy and sounding the latest position of the shifting sandbars. *Defiant*, with her 4 ½ foot draft, can successfully navigate and anchor inside. The wide, main entry channel, 6 to 8 feet deep, is on the southeast side between the Gull Keys and the largest island. East of this channel, numerous coral heads grow in shallow water.

Local fishermen are frequent visitors to the area, but we only spotted one during our late spring jaunt. Nature lovers are thrilled to explore the convoluted mangrove coves and creeks. The diamondback terrapin turtle, sea turtles, crab, wading birds, tropical hardwoods and flora, all thrive here. Soft, sandy beaches are on the north and eastern outer edges of the Marquesas ring. A distance offshore on the west side is the treasure recovery zone of the famous Mel Fisher.

After years of frustration and searching, Fisher and his team uncovered some lost cargo from a fleet of loot-laden Spanish galleons that were defeated by stormy weather a few hundred years ago. Legend has it that earlier treasure salvagers had hidden a stash of recovered Spanish booty in the Marquesas. It may be a myth, but a number of years ago some people were in serious legal trouble after attempting to locate and dig up the alleged cache.

Seagoing outlaws, who lurked along the Keys island chain during their swashbuckling moment in history, supposedly camped or hid here. Pirate artifacts may be scattered in the sands, perhaps to be uncovered in the next blustery storm.

Some say the Marquesas, with its doughnutty shape, was birthed by a meteor impact. Mulling over that idea, I wondered if there were any extraterrestrial mineral fragments deeply concealed in the sands along with the salvager's supposed treasure and antique pirate refuse. In more recent history, the Navy had used the area for target practice. Today, it's not uncommon to find an empty, barnacle-encrusted bomb shell washed up on the beach.

The tide had fallen too far for us to approach the easterly islands and investigate what looked like small, home made boats abandoned onshore. The location was too sheltered to be random beaching of flotsam and the boats surely had some stories to tell. Cuban refugees occasionally find the Marquesas and traces of their successful landings, including encampments, have been found by other visitors.

Intrigued into a contemplative silence, we walked along the sandy shore, while sandpipers were squeaking and scurrying around us like overcharged wind up toys. They were having a productive time securing edibles exposed by the falling tide. On that note, we returned to Bill's boat for a picnic lunch.

The interest, however, isn't just relegated to the Marquesas isles and its lagoon. Snorkel and dive worthy wrecks lie just offshore. One deteriorated ship protrudes, skeleton-like, above the water's surface, and many wrecks are uncharted. Take care since the current outside the Marquesas can be unexpectedly strong at times.

An escape into this tranquil ring of isles, rich with legend and nature, is a memorable experience. Knowing the history of the Marquesas makes a visit even more fascinating. The possibility of a seascape shaping space rock, lost treasure, maritime bandits, and intrepid Cuban refugees had indeed fueled the fires of our imaginations.

Fair weather is the best time to explore, and favorable sailing is most available in the spring and late fall. Summer season typically requires motoring, but the seas are calm aside from the isolated and usually short lived thunderstorm.

With the exception of what hurricane season may produce, winter brings the most dangerous weather with blustery cold fronts that induce long term bouts of rough seas and high winds. Winter season is the least conducive to snorkeling and safe eyeball navigation in the Keys.

Bug screens for after dark, plenty of water and provisions, and updated charts will aid in the comfort factor should one pay this area a visit. A camera and a kayak, or similar, to unobtrusively pass through the shallows and admire the area's tenants also enhances the appreciation for what's truly valuable in our fragile world.

33

Loosing the Cruise: Hurricane Hideout Hustle

It was early summer, 2005. Bill and I had saved our earnings and prepared our vessels as tourism season came to a close and cruising season neared. Earning less that year, we delayed traveling and extended our work schedules. Our sailing goals were delayed even further as a pushy tropical storm bubbled toward the Caribbean in early July. As tropical storm Dennis whipped itself into a hurricane southeast of Jamaica, *Defiant* and *Angel* disregarded any plan of cruising and scrambled for cover.

Boat owners in the hurricane belt need to have a personalized storm plan. Some haul out, others head for marinas and some run for the trees. Since there were so many mangrove islands and rivers in southwest Florida, Bill and I tended to favor the cruiser's trick of hiding in natural, tree-lined canals. Captain Bill gets the credit for showing me the duck for cover in the trees trick. The key to survival is to stay ahead of the weather, act early, avoid unsafe risk taking, and use plenty of common sense.

Acting early, we tucked our boats in a narrow, mangrove framed river and prepared them for potential high winds. Anchors were strung out and lines were secured to the thickest, strongest looking tree trunks. Old towels and canvas wrap padded the trunks from potential chafe by our ropes.

Once our sailboats were secured, we killed time by socializing in *Defiant's* cabin and anxiously pondering our unwelcome situation. We distracted ourselves by watching a movie. Before we knew it, night had fallen and I was ready to return to *Angel.*

On *Defiant's* deck and looking down at *Squishy*, I hesitated. Dark, tangled branches reared like claws over a black river of water. Something unseen behind us made a hoarse croaking noise. Bugs, or perhaps tree frogs, trilled in the trees. The hot, humid air smelled heavily of brine. Silent lightning flashed in the distant skies.

"Uhm, I didn't bring a flashlight," I said, biting my lip. Bill ducked below, rustled about, and returned.

"Here, use this, it's a spare." He clicked a small flashlight on and shone it toward *Angel.* Only about 50 yards away, her curvy yellow stern gleamed in the inky darkness down the channel. "Shine the light on the water," Bill instructed. "Like this, see?"

"On the water?" Foot dangling, I began lowering myself into *Squishy.*

"Uh-huh, pay attention now," Bill said, jiggling the flashlight. "There might be saltwater crocodiles out there and you have to be careful."

"What!" I bounced back on *Defiant's* deck.

"Just use the flashlight. You'll be able to see the shine from their eyes." He demonstrated by sweeping the flashlight around the dark water. "There's none here. Their eyes glow red in the light so they're easy to spot."

"There are crocodiles? With glowing red eyes? Are you kidding me!" Creeping backwards, I bumped into *Defiant's* mizzen mast. Bill had an aptitude for playfully kidding with me, but there really were crocodiles, especially around the nearby Ten Thousand Islands and in the Everglades. It wasn't impossible for them to wander where we were hiding.

"It'll be okay, I'll keep an eye on you. Then you radio me as soon as you get into *Angel.*"

I swallowed and took the flashlight. "All right," I said weakly, forcing myself to board *Squishy*. Outboard roaring, I sloppily veered toward *Angel*, the beam of Bill's flashlight wobbling all over the place to assure there were no glowing red eyes. Once aboard *Angel*, I hastily locked myself in, secured all hatches, and radioed Bill.

"I'm okay!" I said breathlessly.

"Good," Bill radioed back. "It's pretty scary out there."

I thought for a moment, and then slyly narrowed my eyes. "What about Florida panthers? And snakes! With all those snakes in the Everglades, some may've migrated here. And there's got to be spiders here." I knew that Bill hated spiders.

"Panthers would have to swim to get here," Bill said. "And then there's nothing for them to eat."

"Cats can swim," I said. "And they could eat the birds here. They're probably really hungry though and are sneaking through the trees, looking at us."

"That's not funny."

On July 7th, the lower Florida Keys were under a mandatory evacuation and Monroe county declared a state of emergency for its population. Draw bridges were locked down as an endless stream of vehicles poured out of the single road leading up the Keys. Dennis was swirling closer as a category three hurricane and would soon blossom into a category four. Long, impatient lines formed at island gas stations. Grocery stores were mobbed and the bottled water isles quickly emptied. The local booze stores were also running out of stock.

"I didn't sleep so good last night," Bill admitted. Miles away from the municipal chaos, we could only sit on our sailboats and entertain ourselves. "Something jumped on *Defiant's* cabin late last night and I swore it was a panther. I thought it was going to come through the bug screen, so I put the pin boards in, which made it hot all night, even with the fan. Then I realized it was just a heron." Moustache bristling, he squinted at me.

I cleared my throat to stifle a chuckle. "Well, at least it wasn't a crocodile with red eyes."

"You were messing with me!" He pushed my arm. "You had me paranoid all night."

"I think we were both paranoid all night."

The next evening, we secured ourselves in our cabins, the winds beyond the trees now gusting to 44 miles per hour. Inside the shelter of the trees, the winds were mild. There were no waves above a small chop since there was little fetch in our narrow, dogleg channel. We were also surrounded by shallow tidal flats.

However, our masts were sticking out beyond the tree's protection and they felt the true wind, our boats jolting and twitching to each gust. Approaching rapidly, Dennis was blasting over Cuba. Soon, the winds around us would roar into the 60's and 70's. I took a hot shower before things degenerated and became too unstable.

"Do you have a light on?" Bill radioed in the late evening. I told him I had a cabin light on. "There are lights in the mangroves, do you see them?" I peered out of a port window. Hundreds of green glowing specks of light were swirling and blinking within the trees.

I cast a suspicious glance at the cup of partially consumed wine next to a half-eaten donut. It was an odd combination, but what the heck. There was a hurricane outside our port windows.

"Those look like lightning bugs," Bill said.

"Holy cow, they are!" I stared out into the darkness for a while, wondering why the bugs weren't hiding. The growing winds beyond started to sound like a jet engine and *Angel* jerkily rocked from side to side. Static began to hiss in the background of the FM radio station I had on.

"It's going to be a long night," said Max Mayfield, a well known weather expert, as he provided the station with storm updates. Unable to sleep, I certainly agreed with Max. The station also had locals calling in, many of them sounding drunk, to relay what they were experiencing. Then, after a burst of static, the radio went silent. Alarmed, I checked *Angel's* power, but she was fine.

After a long, uncomfortable silence, the FM radio station crackled back to life. "...on emergency power right now," said the DJ. He proceeded to describe how the station's roof was leaking. Next, the National Weather Service VHF broad cast went silent. I twirled the knob and pushed a few buttons. Nothing.

Angel's VHF radio buzzed. "You still there?" Capt. Bill said.

"Yeah," I said, and added, "I can't get the weather."

Bill came back. "They're off the air. Their power must be out." To pass the time, Bill and I nervously chattered on the radio while our sailboats rattled in the gusty winds. The eye of hurricane Dennis swung to our west.

"Why do these things always have to happen at night?" Bill lamented. "And what really ⬛⬛⬛...I ran out of M&Ms."

Our rigs began producing eerie fluting sounds as our sailboats were roughly rattled by the uneven winds. Outside, lion like roaring noises increased in pitch. A rivulet of rain tricked down the front of my mast, which was shaking nonstop, inside the cabin. I made a mental note to fix the leak when it was safe to do so.

By the next morning, the storm had passed. The channel was littered with leaves, branches, and other floating debris. The water was white with stirred up silt. Though stained with mangrove leaves, our boats were okay. We were okay. A Coast Guard rescue helicopter flew past, its passenger looking down at us.

Bill and I had canceled our cruising plans for this year and instead focused on running away from storms. Near the end of August, a subtle weather pattern developing in the tropics was inciting a sense of unease. A mere tropical depression, Katrina didn't have a name yet, and it was a hot, sunny and windless day. The weather forecast was mild and raised no brows.

Nevertheless, I hastily stuffed my bowsprit into another lonely mangrove channel. *Defiant* settled nearby. Bill, falling back on nearly a lifetime of professional experience at sea, didn't like the looks of the skies. I was relying on something much harder to explain.

A wise elder, my grandmother had taught me things that were at one time everyday life in her past. One of these beliefs is that everything has a spirit, even manmade things like homes and boats. One could learn from and communicate with that spirit. Of course, these traditional ways are no substitutes for practical seamanship, but I couldn't resist including these beliefs in what I do.

Though modern society may question my less-modern approach, it's not an option for me to ignore native traditions that are many thousands of years old. Between Bill's serious nautical experience and my belief that *Angel's* spirit urgently wanted to hide, we had dropped everything to run away in perfectly fine weather. Two days later, Hurricane Katrina crossed over South Florida. Surprised citizens had little chance to prepare.

Katrina swiftly swept along the Keys chain, intensifying as it progressed. It came at night with torrential rains and tornadoes. Unable to sleep, I tried to make coffee as *Angel* was being bodily shaken like a toy in the hands of a hyperactive kid. It's sort of like when someone shakes a can of nuts to see how many are left. There was only one nut inside *Angel*.

A lone boater on the VHF radio who was anchored in Key West's harbor area was stuck on his vessel during the storm. Voice panicky, he reported that the waves in the anchorage were breaking over his deck. He watched four boats wash up on Fleming Key. A few sailboats near him lost their masts. With winds howling in the 70s, an 86 mile an hour gust was recorded whipping through Key West. Katrina was the fourth wettest storm in this area since record keeping began in 1871.

To our relief, the boater on the VHF had hung in there, terrified but unharmed. Though sheltered in the trees, *Defiant's* masthead antenna tore away and *Angel's* saggy old bimini self destructed because I'd failed to take it down. Even though we'd hid, we hadn't actually believed that Katrina would become much.

When it was safe enough, I took the dinghy over to *Defiant* to share dinner and watch a movie. As Bill had gotten to know me, he'd learned about my cultural beliefs. He liked the idea that a boat's spirit could possibly be listened to and learned from, especially if it's advantageous to one's safety. I told him that it didn't matter what one's background or heritage was. Anyone can freely choose to learn and apply this sensitivity while cruising or to daily life. It's just a matter of being open minded and attentive to one's natural intuition. Still, the subject was awkward for me to talk about.

It's easy to say that a decision was made based on practical experience. It's not so easy to admit that I took an action because a certain yellow sailboat "talks" to me about it. If one openly shares such uncommon things in this society, men in white suits and a rubber van might just pay a visit. Still, a mariner has to use all options available to keep one's life and property safe. Sometimes that means thinking and seeing outside of the box.

After four long days in the trees, Bill and I were so bored that we were watching crabs crawl around the nearby mangrove roots. Oddly, we started racing them while making bets. Katrina had stirred the water so badly that we couldn't see our escape channel. The snaking route was surrounded by shallow tidal flats, which we couldn't see either. By the fifth day, and heedless of the water clarity, *Angel* and *Defiant* ran in a hasty panic away from the mangroves.

Activated by the hurricane's rains, swarms of biting bugs had made the trees nearly intolerable. *Defiant* managed to make it all the way to the channel's entrance before promptly running aground on a falling tide. Resorting to my depth sounder and tuned to *Angel's* lively spirit, I stayed in deeper water. There were no markers in the convoluted channel. Reading the water's current flow was difficult in the post-storm swell and chop. The winds were a steady twenty knots.

Angel and I were almost free when Bill, trying to be helpful, radioed. "You're gonna run aground over there!

Turn west." *Angel* did not want to turn west. Uncertain whether to listen to an experienced sea captain or to my sailboat, I swerved like a drunken ice skater. Flashing different readouts, the depth sounder gave up and blinked in confusion.

"No, no, turn west!" Bill urged. *No, no turn east, Angel* seemed to say. Conflicted, I turned west. Bumping to a halt, *Angel* joined *Defiant*. Boom drooping in defeat, she slowly leaned over like a wounded animal. Don't tell the men in the rubber van, but I really should've listened to my sailboat.

The high tide went out and wouldn't return for a long 24 hours. *Defiant* and *Angel* were resting on their bilges at a 30-degree angle in silt and sand. Anchors had been strung out on both vessels. The water was only ankle deep, and I found it disconcerting to see *Angel's* nether regions completely exposed. When I crawled inside the cabin, I began to feel sick. I didn't throw up, but *Angel* wasn't so lucky. She managed to expel the contents of her freshwater tank.

At least I had a spare jerry jug with some water in it. Adding insult to injury, a loud thunderstorm with tropical storm force winds rumbled our way. With pelting rain, the weather came and kicked us while we were down. After the storm, I walked *Squishy* over to *Defiant* to see how Bill was doing. We tried to make sandwiches in the ketch's tilted galley without letting the food slide to the floor. It was impossible to set anything down. Bill was still hunting for a lost handful of M&Ms, the small candies wedged in illogical areas of his cabin.

Later, in the middle of the night, *Angel* was partially buoyed by the incoming tide. I was soon able to kedge free and anchor in the channel to wait for first light. *Defiant* floated free just before dawn. Finally, we were bounding through the refreshingly deeper waters of the Gulf. Aside from scuffed bottom paint, both boats were unharmed. We raced toward Key West.

While I was helming *Angel* and gazing at the waters ahead, I suddenly felt something prickly and clammy clamp over my arm. Dismayed, I turned my head and was face to face with a seagull. It dumbly sat there, blinking at me, webbed feet clutching my arm.

"Ah!" I yelped and *Angel* veered off course, mainsail flapping. The gull winged away.

"Are you okay?" Bill radioed.

"A bird scared me," I explained, feeling obtuse, tugging on the mainsheet and struggling to regain *Angel's* course.

"Birds act weird after storms," Bill explained.

"I act weird *during* storms."

We found our way into Key West and managed to rest and regain our senses just in time for Hurricane Rita in September. Once more, *Angel* had talked me into another wild ride into mangrove no man's land. Rita wasn't as ferocious as the others, but we'd rather be overcautious than damaged.

To continue the trend of once-a-month hurricane visitations, hurricane Wilma tightened into a freakish category five in late October as it wobbled toward the Yucatan. Once again, *Defiant* and *Angel* were in the trees with the no-see-ums, crabs, and mosquitoes. Wilma's speed and path was unpredictable, and its projected arrival in our area was delayed as it caused frightful damage to Mexico in the Yucatan.

"We'll be up here in bug land longer," Bill said, waving at imaginary insects.

"At least we've got extra beers and stuff," I said, rapping my knuckles on the cooler in *Defiant's* cockpit. Our vessel's refrigerators were small and packed with abundant food, so we'd stocked up on ice and beer after learning from our earlier hurricane dodging efforts.

This time we had something more interesting to do to pass the time. Bill and I were creating a giant, purple dragon costume for a popular Key West event at the end of October. It looked as if Wilma would delay this event, but that didn't stop us from making costumes for this famous festival.

We enjoyed volunteering during this time and had developed a routine of entertaining tourists and locals. Mostly, we performed humorous skits with our giant stage creations at the Pier House Resort. Since *Defiant* had the most room, Bill got to store the nearly completed dragon costume in his forward cabin.

As Wilma roared through the night, *Angel* and *Defiant* weathered the familiar routine of sonorous noises and pelting storm bands. We also heard what sounded like human voices outside as Wilma's violent eye wall squalled overhead.

Bill wondered if it was some sort of feedback from his VHF radio, but the sounds were still heard when he momentarily turned the unit off. On *Angel*, I was sure I'd heard Bill calling my name and laughing. He insisted he'd done no such thing and admitted that he thought I was shouting his name and laughing.

"Once again, it comes at night," Bill radioed. He was huddled in *Defiant's* aft cabin. He heard what sounded like his boat's front hatch slam open and was compelled to investigate. He dashed outside in *Defiant's* center cockpit. Exposed to the dark, howling weather, he struggled to access the main cabin.

Ducking low and protected by *Defiant's* cockpit coaming, he entered the front cabin. Wet from the cold rain, he carefully descended the companionway steps. He felt his way around in the darkness. The wind was shrieking and lightning flashed, briefly illuminating the head of a wide eyed monster. The head was swiveling around in the rocking boat, rows of conical white teeth in gaping, dark jaws.

Bill yowled and backed into the ladder. Lightning flashed and boomed again, and Bill saw the monster's fake, purple fur. He'd forgotten about the giant dragon costume. Its head and neck had been shaken loose from its ties in the cabin's corner and was loosely flailing about. Laughing at himself, Bill locked his hatch and secured the unruly costume.

In Key West, weather measuring instruments were damaged by the winds. Before they were disabled, they were measuring gusts in the 80 mile per hour range. By the wee hours of the morning, our ropes that had been tied to the tree trunks, normally above cockpit level, were underwater. The power went out in the lower and middle Keys. The winds around us began to ease as Wilma, a massive 460 miles across, retreated.

"…and we are slowly going underwater," said a local who'd called into the FM radio station, which, presumably, was on emergency power. There were no other stations on the air.

"You see outside?" Bill radioed. "It looks like another planet out there!" It was safe enough to venture out. In the dim, gray light of an occluded sunrise, I slackened the lines that secured *Angel* to the trees. They steeply angled down, the trees partly submerged in the rising storm tide.

The thick air was saturated with a salt haze. A mayonnaise container floated past. Above, a ruffled looking bald eagle glided over our masts. A few small boats, dislodged from their anchoring areas from who knows where, had been blown against the mangroves on the other side of our hiding spot.

Several days later, we returned to Key West. The anchoring areas were nearly empty and debris floated everywhere; pieces of docks, pieces of boats, branches, and a lawn chair. Numerous cars, businesses, and homes in this area had suffered from Wilma's unexpectedly high storm tide. Backyard swimming pools had fish in them and locals were finding sea life lodged in trees. The whole scene was chaotic. It was akin to the hectic activity of ants after they suffer the indignity of having their hill kicked over.

The Keys islands eventually recovered and by next season, *Defiant* and *Angel* had returned to their usually scheduled cruising program. Creatures of routine, we worked and participated in the community, saved money, and then cruised. We were so impressed by the beauty of the out islands that we returned to the same ones for several more seasons. What especially drew us to trace the same path was the chance to see our friends again, both locals and other boaters.

* * *

SECTION TWO

The Wordy How and Why

Escaping the "system," living aboard,
and self sufficiency

Leaving the Rat Race
Learning to Sail
Becoming a Liveaboard Traveler
Liveaboard Basics

34

Why Boats? A Brief Background

Before they'd separated, my parents were living close to Lake Michigan in a rural area just north of Milwaukee, Wisconsin. They were hard working folk, descendents of fisherman, sailors, and a seafood loving tribe of natives from the Arctic Circle. Several of our relatives had been lost at sea, most while working in the Great Lakes. My mom's father, a sailor, plied the Great Lakes on cargo ships when he lived in Milwaukee as a young man.

Understandably, both of my parents choose to work ashore, mostly. Dad was a mechanic, construction worker, and fisherman. Mom waitressed then found her niche working in sales at a local newspaper. They always seemed to be taking time off from work ashore to head out on the water in a small fishing boat. Dad's alternate occupation was fishing and he did it constantly.

When they'd brought me into the world, their avid marine life didn't change. My water loving parents simply brought me, and plenty of baby supplies, along. I was raised in two worlds: on fishing boats and in an old, countryside house.

When poking around the Great Lakes shoreline, my parents favored natural areas. They'd often dock or beach the boat to go hiking and camping. I treasure the memories of hiking with my grandfather where he'd show us a smorgasbord of wild fruits, nuts, and plants that his ancestors would gather. This fostered an appreciation, and a need, to be close to nature.

Five years later, my sister Krista was born and I had a fascinating new playmate. When Krista was old enough, our parents took us to ports beyond the Great Lakes. Through our parents, we were introduced to the amazing, jewel-like waters of the Bahamas, Central America, and Caribbean.

Though working class, mom and dad had saved and set aside funds for boating adventures that some believe only the rich are privy to. A part of me must've remained behind on those enchanting, sandy shored islands, ensuring a return when I was older and able to do so.

35

The Mid 1990s: The End and Beginning

After simultaneously attending college fulltime and working fulltime on a factory assembly line that produced condoms, amongst other things, I was soon drawn into a fast paced life of materialism. Because of working long hours early in life, I'd saved money for finding my own place. As a young adult, I had a new engineering career and the responsibilities of home ownership. My house was a single level dwelling in a friendly neighborhood along the edge of a Wisconsin town called West Bend.

Milwaukee, less than an hour's drive away, is highly industrial. Harley Davidson, Briggs & Stratton, Rockwell Automation, and Johnson Controls are just some of the familiar names that have grown out of the area's industriousness. Other well known names such as John Deere, Mercury Marine, Kohler, and Kimberly Clark (the maker of goods such as Huggies, Kleenex and Kotex) were located a few hours away from Milwaukee.

180

I worked in the engineering, design, and testing departments of a manufacturing plant. I was a tiny cog in a great, hectic wheel that turned out a variety of household consumer goods. Its immense factory floor was a maze of clamoring machinery, shouting supervisors, and workers.

Life revolved around a strict work schedule, mortgage and car payments, traffic jams, television, and learning what status symbols were. Most of my peers were into "getting ahead" and urged me to do the same. I had no idea what this actually meant, but it had certainly had something to do with being financially and materially successful. The whole concept was empty and meaningless. I adored my coworkers and friends, but felt uncertain about the "getting ahead" motive.

Social expectations had strongly influenced me to behave a certain way, so I'd tried to satisfy those obligations at my own expense. I'd mistakenly started young adulthood by being more concerned about meeting social norms, and worried about what other people thought. I hadn't been shown how to discover what I really wanted in life. I enjoyed working and needed to keep busy, but, deep down; I'd rather have a job I truly enjoyed.

Restless, feeling suffocated by the path I'd taken, I developed a secretive habit of looking at boats. Visiting marinas, I wistfully gazed at the older power boats, ones that were similar to the vessels I was raised on, and fantasized about white sands and turquoise seas. It seemed the ancestral connection to the sea had come back to haunt me. Mired in home ownership and career, I felt even greater unrest when my mom and sister relocated to southwest Florida near the Everglades. Their move inspired me to entertain the alluring idea of a year round boating season.

At home, shelves gradually overflowed with magazines and books about boating, both power and sail.

Internet searches and virtual boater's chat rooms only fueled my restlessness. Believing that I'd get the boating bug out of my system by spending some time on the water, I joined a community sailing center. Seemingly thrilled to have a power boater who was curious about sailboats, my new friends on the water went out of their way to teach me about sailing. I loved it. Something had been started and there was no stopping it.

Encouraged by what I'd learned at the sailing center, and having so much fun, I purchased a 16-foot trailerable sailing trimaran. The sleek looking vessel, called a Windrider, was made by Wilderness Systems. Inspired by a near relative with Russian Cossack ancestry, I named the three-hulled vessel *Troika*. Whenever I had a spare moment, I was out on Lake Michigan or on one of Wisconsin's numerous inland lakes, rain or shine.

On *Troika*, I was free from the suffocating realm of uptight managers, material pursuits, and bills. After two seasons of enjoying my little trimaran, the boating bug only worsened. It didn't help that the owners of larger boats from the sailing center kept inviting me to crew on their vessels. Now I was lusting after a bigger boat, something sturdy that was big enough to live in. My land based social circle, doubting my sanity by this time, insisted I'd have to save up and wait for retirement in order to make that fantasy a reality.

I despised the concept of having to wait for retirement in order to enjoy life. Why not own a live aboard boat sooner, while I was young enough to enjoy it, rather than later? However, there was a catch. I could only afford a larger vessel and associated marina fees if I continued working the long days my job typically demanded. That left no time for enjoying and caring for a live aboard. There was barely enough time to crew on friend's boats or for having fun with *Troika*. If I reduced work hours in order to have the time needed to enjoy my own cruising vessel, then I wouldn't be able to afford both the house and a boat. Something had to give.

Faced with that seemingly inescapable dilemma, a course of action was required. Being raised in a society where hard work's a virtue, and devotion to the community is placed over one's own needs and interests, I felt selfish. I was expected to appreciate the hard won material goods surrounding me, though such things were meaningless and artificial. I was supposed to be glad I had a stable career, even though I didn't really enjoy it. My social environment hinted it was too self serving to drop off the path of conformity to consider or pursue one's own happiness. An understanding and much wiser coworker named Gail helped break this unproductive view.

"What's so selfish about wanting to be happy? If you're not happy, you can't make others happy. That's just stupid." Gail said. "Change isn't easy, but better now than later! Get with it, girl. What's the point if you're not happy, dum dum! What if you die tomorrow – I'm just saying – and then what?"

Her words helped me see the light. If I'm doing something that is truly meaningful to me, I'd be more capable of sharing that positivity with others. If I had a job I actually enjoyed and cared about, I'd certainly be a more productive member of the community. Instead of just going through the motions like some automaton, I'd be more true to others as well as to myself. I'd better start taking charge of my own life and following my own vision instead of what a particular segment of society dictated.

As Gail had said, change isn't easy. Quitting a career with a secure future and taking odd jobs with less pay and less hours goes against everything I'd been taught. Trading home ownership for a live aboard boat was, by mainstream society's standards, irresponsible. Nevertheless, it was liberating to allow myself to cease worrying about how others thought I should live my life. With a new sense of purpose, I searched for a cruising sailboat.

36

Single Female Seeking Strong Monohull With Seagoing Experience. Must Weigh More Than Three Tons. Nonsmoking Diesel Preferred.

Thanks to all the obsessive reading and research I'd done, I knew what I wanted in a boat. My idea of a good sailboat would be cutter rigged and easy to set up for singlehanding. With the primary intent of coastal cruising and sight seeing, she'd have a shoal draft with a full keel. Her mast would be keel-stepped for sturdiness and she'd be thickly built out of low maintenance fiberglass, strong and able to handle the inevitable storm.

Of course, she would be pleasing to the eye and small enough to afford upkeep, yet large enough to be comfortable living in. I'd selected sail over power for economic reasons and for the lesser environmental impact. Using the wind for propulsion, with occasional use of a small diesel inboard, and generating electrical power primarily with solar panels, would at least be greener than how I was living at the moment. While I searched, I restlessly kept up with the usual life of work, debts, and traffic jams.

One of my long distance boating friends who communicated via the internet, Captain Bill Robinson, had been especially active in helping me search for potential cruising boats. Mariners love helping their fellows, especially a newbie like me. He spotted something called a Bayfield Cutter in an online ad, pointed her out and urged me to go see her. The fact that she was a freshwater boat from the Great Lakes, my own sailing backyard, piqued some interest. However, I was unimpressed with the ad, which was full of misspellings and demanded a steep asking price.

The ad curtly stated the boat was "in fin cond" and "just haulded." The grainy, black and white photo of this mystery boat, which looked like some frightened creature huddled in the corner of an oversize slip, was unflattering. Since she was not too far from another boat that I had an appointment to see, I added the Bayfield Cutter to the list.

Finally finding the right cruising boat can be like an awkward first date. I didn't know why *Angel* made me feel so nervous, but she did. It was because I knew that she was mine from the moment I saw her weathered bowsprit at the far end of the dock. She was a Bayfield 29 cutter with a customized extended platform bowsprit that gave her an overall length of a reasonable 31 feet. Anything longer would present more of a financial challenge to maintain.

The boat had everything I'd been hoping for. She had a heavy duty keel-stepped aluminum mast and a thick fiberglass hull that had been laid up by hand. Her full keel had encapsulated ballast, a cut away forefoot, and a 3 ½-foot deep shoal draft. The Bayfield was cutter rigged, meaning that she had two headsails and a main. In addition, her traditional lines and clipper ship's bow, with carved wooden trail boards no less, made her incredibly attractive. Buoyant, sporting a bright yellow paint job, she looked far better than that pitiable, black and white photo in the ad. I couldn't stop staring.

Naturally, there was a catch. Built in Ontario, Canada, in 1978, *Angel* had been sitting and aging for a long time. Though sound of hull, deck and rig, her diesel engine was on its last leg, and she was a cosmetic catastrophe. She was also remarkably deficient in the electrical and boating accessory department.

She didn't even have an anchor and chain, or basic safety gear, and her mainsail had holes in it. *Angel's* freshwater plumbing needed attention and rowdy birds had to be evicted from her cockpit. Eager to sell, the owner dramatically dropped his asking price, but much would be spent on equipping her. I saw this as an opportunity to learn, hands on, about a larger vessel's repair and upkeep.

This was it. I quit my job and sold all but the most basic possessions. Debts, including college tuition loans, were paid off and I used the remaining funds toward building a new life with *Angel*. (Ridiculously sentimental about boats, I did keep *Troika*, storing her at a small sailing club for a modest fee.) Everything was changing completely and there was no easy return. My life would never be the same. I'd been freed from a path that had been suffocating my ability to grow, truly enjoy life, and learn about who I really was.

After a shopping spree in a boating supply store, *Angel* was equipped with the basic necessities for safe travel. We headed south toward my family while fine tuning the new girl-sailboat relationship. All the obsessive reading, communication with other mariners, time spent on *Troika*, sailing lessons, and crewing on big boats at the sailing center provided an invaluable foundation. That background instilled a sense of confidence that would only increase as I got to know my boat and gain some experience with her.

Ancient, single cylinder diesel rattling, backing out of the slip in a cloud of exhaust, *Angel* chugged away on a calm, clear day. That was the start of a new life of seasonal cruising and living aboard. I never looked back.

37

To the Florida Keys

Free and mobile, I sought a home port that would allow me to sail year round. My mom and sister, though baffled by my radical life change, had encouraged me to swing their way near Naples, on the southwest coast of Florida. I was more than ready. No hesitating, no lingering, just hurry up, go as fast as I could, and get far away from my old material life. Sights set on the sunny south, the northeast receded behind me.

Not too far from family, and based in the Florida Keys, was Captain Bill Robinson, the mariner who had found *Angel's* ad and was responsible for bringing me and her together. During my career focused years in Wisconsin, I'd enjoyed socializing with Bill on an internet site where veteran cruising boaters and new hopefuls like me developed camaraderie, swapped stories, and sought or gave advice.

Capt. Bill was intrigued by the possibility of having an enthusiastic new cruising boater, a young female besides, migrate to his home port. He encouraged me to come and see it in person. Years ago, I'd been to the Florida Keys just once, by boat, and that was with my parents. All I recalled were shallow, but amazingly translucent waters and the aggressive commercialism of Key West. Happy to help, Bill didn't mind going out of his way to meet me.

After visiting mom, *Angel* was ready to sail toward the lower Florida Keys. Riding an easy breeze between the Gulf of Mexico and Florida Bay, I watched a stocky, blue two-masted sailboat purposefully veer toward me. Pushing and pulling the tiller, I swung *Angel* from side to side. The ketch responded in kind and then swished past me, her bow pushing a foaming, hissing curl of water. Her lone sailor was grinning. It was Captain Bill, eager to lead me into his territory. A fishing guide by trade, Bill lived aboard and traveled in his ketch, a 36 foot antique Morgan Out Island named *Defiant*. She'd been built in 1974, four years earlier than my own boat.

I slowly tacked, sails flapping, bowsprit rising and falling in a mild swell. Tacking, or changing direction with one's bow into the wind, in a sailboat with a wide body and three sails, took some practice. I enjoyed the mild challenge. Manipulating the sheets, or ropes, that controlled the sails necessitated some coordination. I had to tighten both sheets that lead to the two headsails and manipulate *Angel's* twin mainsail sheets while simultaneously pushing on the tiller.

Downwind, *Defiant* expertly gybed, the sun-touched seas glittering around her. *Angel's* staysail and yankee winches buzzed as I pulled in their sheets without using the winch handles, then cleated them. Hardware clinking on aluminum, the mainsail's boom swung into the new tack. Aged, perforated sails filling, *Angel* heeled and accelerated. Blue

With his military background, Bill was more traveled and had the advantage of seniority in years and experience. Though open minded, he couldn't help but struggle to take me seriously and wonder how long I'd last living on a boat. As reasonable adults, we realized that we had to give our friendship time to evolve and grow. Bill had to learn to trust my capabilities and I had to learn not to get defensive over this natural, human process. Meanwhile, we discussed a mutually fascinating subject; cruising and boats.

38

Plan for Adventure, Now!

Settling in the Keys, I anchored near *Defiant* and worked on *Angel*. The priority was having her sailing gear and living comforts up to my own picky standard. I wasn't fond of the boat's existing shower system, which consisted of a small, plastic bag that hung overhead, was heated by the sun, and sprinkled lukewarm water. It is one thing to use these temporarily while camping, but I didn't want to permanently live with it. The bag's water would turn green with algae and it was awkward to fill. Before arriving in the Keys, *Angel* was kept in marinas, which offer household style showers.

I fell back on the engineering background to construct a hot water tank and solar collector with a fold away indoor shower stall in the bow. Instead of a traditional V-berth sleeping bunk, the Bayfield 29 had a head, boat talk for the bathroom, in her bow. The sleeping bunk was a generous area on her starboard, right hand, side. *Angel's* compact living areas reminded me of the RV that my

194

mom's old boyfriend once had. Like the RV traveler, I didn't mind residing in small spaces and preferred to keep possessions at a minimum.

To earn a living, I wasn't quite sure what I'd do. When I wasn't working on *Angel*, I began a series of small paintings on canvas. During my late teen years and after some college coursework in illustration and graphics, painting became an avid hobby. Bill told me that tourism driven areas like Key West appreciate the creative arts and selling some paintings in a local gallery or consignment store was a possibility. Key West's downtown Duval Street had a plethora fine galleries and shops.

Working as a visual artist was also an opportunity for social involvement in the form of art exhibits, street fairs, and volunteering. Just because I ran off on a sailboat didn't mean I was trying to avoid the responsibility of work or social interaction.

The island community was mostly friendly and connections were soon established. At that time, Key West had only a scattering of mariners who were anchored out and there was no mooring field. During a time from before the mid 1990s to early 2000s, the island adhered to its live-and-let-live attitude and live aboard boaters weren't actively maligned as they are today.

Angel's cracked and absurdly flattened inflatable was unseaworthy, so Bill graciously offered rides to shore until I found a used, but decent fiberglass-bottomed inflatable and outboard. The dinghy, sporting oddly colored patches and never able to completely retain its air, was christened *Squishy*.

In the evenings, we'd socialize and continued to get to know each other. Often, the subject would gravitate toward traveling the waterways, the whole reason we lived aboard boats.

"Is there any place you always wanted to go?" Bill asked. I thought for a moment.

"I'm not sure where to go or if I can afford to go very far right now," I admitted. *Angel* and I could sail in circles and I'd be happy. Though, in the Great Lakes, I'd enjoyed bobbing along natural coastlines and gunkholing, a type of shallow water cruising where boaters seek out isolated and difficult to access areas. Doing the same with sandy, palm fringed tropical coasts was a fantasy I'd always entertained.

"Well, you've got to go somewhere," Bill said. "I always wanted to go to the Bahamas. It's so close. We could just work for the season and then go there during the off season." He waved a hand in a half shrug. "You could pull that off."

"God, I loved the Bahamas." I told Bill about the times my boat loving parents took me there. For some reason, I'd assumed I wouldn't be able to afford to take *Angel* to the Bahamas in my present, uncertain financial state. "Isn't it expensive though?"

Bill slyly cocked a brow. "Not if you anchor out."

The next day, he invited me over to *Defiant* and showed me a chart of the northern Bahamas that he had laminated at the local office center. It was secured over his dining table, completely covering it like a nautical tablecloth. Pushing a fork and a few wayward M&M candies out of the way, he pointed to the spread of tiny islands shown on the chart.

"Every time I sit down to eat, I'll be looking at the Abacos," he said, finger tracing over the Little Bahama Bank. "Soon, I'll have this thing memorized. With her shallow draft, *Defiant* was built to go here." He rounded up the M&Ms that had rolled over Grand Bahama, absently ate them, and then tapped a finger on the far eastern edge of the Abacos. "These specks here are called Out Islands. See? And *Defiant* is a Morgan Out Island."

The next day, I bought a Bahamian chart and tacked it on a bulkhead inside *Angel*. I was intrigued, even a bit intimidated, by the copious scatter of islands with exotic names, located in wide open tracts of shallow water.

Bill and I had spurred each other into setting a real cruising goal. Together we poured over the charts, planning and scheming. We were thrilled by the idea of traveling together instead of alone. This was how the adventure began.

* * *

39

Crossing the Gulf Stream:
Other Boater's Experiences

Boaters heading to the Bahamas from the States must navigate across the Gulf Stream, a small slice of Atlantic that's about 2,500 feet at its steepest depths. Like a great river dividing east Florida and the Bahamas, the Gulf Stream flows with a strong, northerly current, from 1 knot to sometimes just over 3 knots. During my earlier travels, I interviewed other cruisers to hear what the more experienced had to say.

"We hit something," Terry said, smacking one hand into the other. "Bang!" Terry describes a past Gulf Stream crossing with her husband, Captain Ron, and pet poodle, Ocean, on their 36-foot Gulfstream trawler, *Silk Purse IV*.

Every year, thousands of boats cross the Gulf Stream between Florida and the Bahamas. A well worn trail, it's an easy hop when the weather is right. However, when the wind picks up and shifts against the current or squalls start rearing their cloudy heads, a Gulf Stream crossing can be dangerous. Boaters may also encounter fast moving freighters, unlit vessels at night or unseen obstacles floating in the water.

Silk Purse had encountered the latter. It was early summer when the trawler left the north end of Key Biscayne, near Miami, FL, and headed toward Bimini, Bahamas. It was 4 a.m. Experienced travelers, they'd waited for a good weather window and faced less than three-foot seas. In the dim gray light of dawn, *Silk Purse* hit something.

The trawler shuddered as she glanced off a submerged obstacle. Quick-thinking, Ron immediately shifted the engine into neutral while Terry scurried forward. Pushed into motion by *Silk Purse*, a large tree bobbed upright, and then began tumbling end over end. The trawler drifted away. Wide eyed, Terry watched as the tree's massive, tangle of a root ball careened over *Silk Purse's* bow. Just missing the boat's rail, the sodden tree vanished back into the inky water. Undamaged, the lucky trawler was able to continue her journey. With no further surprises, they arrived in Bimini by lunchtime after a 47-nautical mile crossing.

Waiting for good weather, the number of boats in Fort Lauderdale, FL, grew. By Easter weekend, the window opened. *Escape*, a Hunter 290 sloop, bounced and rocked her way through a crazed crowd of weekend warriors, fishing vessels, and fellow Bahamas bound cruisers. It was only 2:30am. Cruising couple Tom and Babette brought *Escape* into calmer seas after skirting a long line of waiting cruise ships. The conditions were so calm that the sailboat motored to West End, Bahamas.

"I would've liked a little wind," Tom admits, but he was glad to finally resume their trip and appreciated its uneventful nature.

"The roughest part of the whole thing was getting through the crowds at Fort Lauderdale!" Babette said. With a 70-nautical mile hop, an early start and fair skies ahead, *Escape* traveled at a fuel conservative pace and reached West End around 3:30pm. Their travel time was 13 hours.

Dennis, a long time sailboat owner, had recently bought *Island Dream*, a trawler. He says he was still thinking like a sailor on his most recent Gulf Stream crossing this June. With his wife, Sharon, and crewmember Bob, Dennis took *Island Dream* out of Jupiter, FL, at 5:00pm for an overnight crossing, 60 nautical miles, to West End. Possessing many years of sailing experience, it was a routine trip for Dennis. However, he was still getting used to his new power vessel's different handling characteristics.

The weather forecast showed nothing alarming. Yet, midway in the trip, a rapidly developing low pressure area formed over *Island Dream*. In the dark of the night, squalls whipped the waves into a dangerous jumble. Easterly winds gusted up to 50 mph, and the growing seas were estimated to be near 12 to 14 feet. About 30 nautical miles offshore, the trawler struggled to make headway.

"At that time, we were only traveling half a knot," Bob says. Forward progress became extremely difficult, and Dennis turned around to make a quick downwind slide to safety. Back in Jupiter, Florida, *Island Dream* waited for better weather to resume her travels, this time by day, and arrived at West End after covering 60 nautical miles in an easy 10 hours.

Dick and Carol Simmons had been crossing the stream every year since 1964 in both power and sailing vessels (and still regularly crossed after that interview). When I was lucky enough to make their acquaintance, they were cruising in *Gusto!!!*, an Island Packet 44. The couple had no trouble recalling their most memorable, and rather harrowing, experience.

It was early fall in the mid-'90s, and they left Port Lucaya, Bahamas, for an 80 nautical mile crossing to Boca Raton, FL. The trip was made overnight, with a favorable forecast. There was no wind and the seas were flat. After a short time, a firm breeze began to build, and *Gusto!!!* rushed along on a broad reach. Dick and Carol became alarmed when the winds continued increasing, hitting 20 knots, and then gusting to 30 knots and beyond. The seas became so steep that a nearby freighter completely disappeared from view whenever it dropped into a wave's trough.

"That was the scariest," Dick admitted, also noting that bad weather at night always seems intensified. "It's hard to see what's coming at you," he says. After a long and difficult sail, *Gusto!!!* landed, in one piece, in Boca Raton after daybreak. Despite that one stormy incident and the many years making crossings, Dick and Carol have had few negative experiences due to careful weather watching and sensible planning.

Calm weather windows are perfect for the cruising trawler while sailboats hope for breezes of up to 15 knots. As expected, sailors prefer to sail across the stream, but most aren't hesitant to take advantage of any good weather window, including calms. It's preferable to be bored and safe than to risk breaking your boat, or yourself. Seasoned mariners will avoid crossing the Gulf Stream if the winds are over 15 knots.

Of course, as *Gusto!!!* and *Island Dream* had experienced, unexpected weather can catch a vessel in the open. Though coincidence, both of these vessels had been traveling at night, when changing skies and unpredictable weather is less visible. The wise captain will avoid crossing the Gulf Stream when the winds have any component of north in them. Northerly winds go against the stream's current as it flows up from the south, and this builds steep and dangerous seas.

From Florida, the most common jump-off points to the Bahamas, usually to West End or to Bimini, are between Key Largo and West Palm Beach, FL. Anything farther north and a vessel is forced to travel against the current, an uncomfortable and uneconomical ride.

Daytime or night crossings are a matter of personal choice and level of experience. Slower vessels will usually plan crossings overnight so they can arrive in the Bahamas with plenty of daylight to spare, enabling them to easily discern deep water from shoals in the clear water. It's a matter of careful planning, plotting, and weather watching.

* * *

40

Eating Underway:
Astronaut Food and Sprout Salad

Boaters are always on the lookout for decent provisions to enjoy during long crossings or weekend cruises. Dining at rest is easy, but eating underway can present a challenge. Strong weather makes cooking difficult and short-handed crews or singlehanders usually don't have the luxury of preparing complete meals while they're sailing.

Hot, savory food is good for morale and brightens a rainy day at sea. Boaters everywhere have the same basic criteria for good eating on the go. Price, refrigeration or not, storage life, quality, taste, serving size, convenience, and dietary concerns are important factors.

While cruising, Bill and I experimented with the self heating meal. The selection earning the highest regard were fairly priced, were heated without using flames or a stove, are not freeze dried, require no refrigeration, have a long shelf life and tasted well. The meal is today's MRE (Meals Ready to Eat). It's not gourmet, but it is food. It works just fine for a boater out in the middle of nowhere whose galley has run out of fresh stock.

Don't let the plain packaging, or past reputation, be a deterrent. Unlike the picturesque wrappings of other brands marketed to the public, with an MRE you're paying for actual product and not for full color ads.

Known as "full moisture pouched food," the idea was born in the 1970s for the U.S. space program. The goal was to provide user friendly meals for astronauts and replace the original and not so appetizing tube style space paste. Soon, the military began using the meals and made them into complete kits for soldiers in the field. Over time, the meals were refined, vastly improving taste and nutritional value. The food pouch can be cooked in a heater bag, dropped in boiling water for several minutes or its pre-cooked contents eaten as is.

The non-flame MRE heater bag makes eating convenient for the boater. A crewman stuck at the helm simply opens the heater bag, inserts the sealed food pouch and then adds a small amount of water. Easy to follow instructions are printed on the packaging. The water reacts with a specially designed pad that contains iron oxide and creates heat without flame.

If the instructions are followed correctly, there is very little water inside the heater bag, so there's no sloshing or boiling water spilling out. The water evaporates as the meal heats, which takes about 10 minutes.

In a rocking boat, I'll wedge the activated heater bag between folded towels in a corner of the cockpit floor while it's cooking. A small amount of metallic-smelling steam slowly vents from the bag, but I didn't find it dangerously hot. The bag will be hot inside though, so be sure to keep curious pets or children out of range.

MRE ingredients can be viewed at www.longlifefood.com. Here, you have the option of purchasing an individual dish or an entire MRE kit. Note that if you order individual entrees, and not the whole kit, you'll need to order the heater bags.

Beef stew, smoked salmon, chicken, chili, ham and shrimp, penne pasta with meatless sausage, and veggie manicotti are some of the offerings. There are also are a variety of breakfasts, sides, desserts, and snacks.

Other full moisture food packages that require no refrigeration are Tasty Bite brand cuisine and Kitchens of India. These quality meals don't come with self heating bags, but can be boiled in their pouches for about five minutes. I have also successfully heated these meals using an MRE heater bag.

Sprouting Fresh Greens

For boaters in the middle of nowhere, fresh greens can be scarce. A simple sprouting jar and bags of sprouting seeds is a healthy addition to the boat's galley. The seeds can be stored for many months.

I obtained a sprouting jar and screened lid, along with instructions on how to do it, from the Handy Pantry health store website. Sealed bags of sprouting seeds, everything from alfalfa and broccoli to bean and lentil seeds were also purchased. All I do is follow the enclosed instructions: soak a few teaspoons of seeds in the sprouting jar and rinse daily. The jar is stored in a clean, safe area. A few days later, the jar is packed with fresh sprouts.

RESOURCES: www.longlifefood.com

www.HandyPantry.com

www.tastybite.com

www.kitchensofindia.com

41

Fishing From a Slow Sailboat

The steady thrum of *Angel's* diesel, compounded by a rhythmic waggle of her hindquarters, was enough to put me into a trance. Unenthused by the lack of wind, my Bayfield drug herself over the glassy clear water. Uneventful weather is always more desirable than stormy seas, but it still made the 65 nautical mile run over Little Bahama Bank tediously long. It was time to break the boredom. I found *Angel's* trolling rig and untangled it, fantasizing about a fish dinner.

Trolling a lure while underway is a worthy endeavor for the marine traveler. After all, part of the appeal of cruising is living life through our own wit and skill as opposed to coddled suppression by society's artificialities. Catching one's own dinner, instead of pulling a packaged, preprocessed meal off a shelf, holds a special satisfaction.

A variety of fish-luring constructions work for trolling. Detailed here is a rugged, basic rig using a spoon lure. Since he's a professional fishing guide with over three decades of experience, Captain Bill was the ideal resource to learn some tricks and techniques of the trade.

While fishing rods work, I don't use one for trolling. Found in Bill's pile of spare parts, a used Penn International II 12T reel was clamped to *Angel's* stern rail so its monofilament line can freely trail astern. A piece of gasket material pads the metal reel to rail connection. 20 to 40 pound test clear monofilament is most commonly used for this type of trolling. The line should be heavier than the target fish, but not too large.

"Fish go for line they can't see," Bill says. "Stealth is the name of the game." Of course, it's also the luck of the draw. There's always the possibility of an oversized fish stripping the line off the reel or breaking the line. Thus, carrying spare mono, lures and accessories is advisable.

A wire leader is needed so fish can't bite through the rig. To suit the spoon lure, *Angel* had two 3-foot lengths of **"Tooth Proof" American Fishing Wire** brand stainless wire, size #9. The wire is tied using a knot called a Haywire Twist. Instructions for this knot are printed on the wire's packaging and it takes some practice to master this tricky, but effective tie. Another popular leader wire is **Surflon** brand nylon coated wire. Though this may seem counterintuitive, a simple overhand knot (not a haywire twist) is used to secure **Surflon**.

Avoid putting kinks in the leader wire and store it by looping in a coil. A toenail cutter or small wire cutters works well for trimming mono and wire ends. To keep the spoon lure from skipping out of the water, a quarter-ounce egg sinker is strung on the leading segment of wire.

A quantity of two size-1 barrel swivels (or size 4 or 5 **'Bill Fisher'** brand ball bearing swivels) was incorporated in the rig, which keeps the fishing line from twisting and breaking. Use black or dull colored swivels and sinkers since fish will nip at anything metallic and shiny. Spoon lures, such as a #3 **Clark Spoon** or similar, preferably with no bead or decorative baubles, are top choices by the pros. The metal lure, when it sits unused for a while, can be polished with WD-40 or similar to keep it gleaming.

"Most lures are designed to catch fishermen, not fish," Bill reminds me. Simple designs work and glitzy additions or rainbow colors aren't necessary for success. The spoon's silver color and wobbling motion is most effective on sunny days and in clear water where fish can see it.

Rubber squid skirt lures are also popular for trolling. For skirts, darker colors, like purples or pinks, are the most successful since the lure's silhouette is what draws the fish's interest. Note that metal spoons last longer than the rubber skirts, which are soon chewed to pieces by fish. The leader-lure assembly is attached to the monofilament with any good fishing knot, such as a swivel hitch or charter boat knot.

The rig was slowly let out behind *Angel* until the lure was about 100 feet from my stern. The drag on the reel was set at a tension where I could just tug the line out with one hand. Note that the drag increases as the line is pulled off the reel and the spool diameter decreases.

The vessel can be strictly sailing, motoring or motor sailing, and trolling speeds of 5 to 7 knots work best for the fish cruisers typically target. The deepwater dorado (also known as dolphin or mahi-mahi), mackerel, small tunas, and snapper from shallower waters, are popular catches.

Some reels have an announcer and will loudly click when a fish pulls the line out. Since mine doesn't, I secured a clothespin near the reel and, keeping the line taut, inserted the mono in the pin's jaws. When a fish strikes, the line is tugged from the clothespin with a hearty snap, an alert that I can hear if the engine is running.

When a fish does hit, let the sails out a little or throttle down just enough to be maintaining slow forward speed. Stopping the boat dead increases the chances of loosing a fish since too much slack can develop in the line, which allows a fish to throw the hook.

The hot sun glared over calm seas during the trip over Little Bahama Bank. Motoring at 5.5 knots, I deployed the trolling rig. I wasn't sure what piscine species, if any, lurked in the sandy-bottomed expanse of shallow water.

As if reading my thoughts, Bill, motoring *Defiant* nearby, radioed, "I doubt there's much out here." Nevertheless, he offered some trolling advice for this type of area. If there were any small islands or underwater features like rocks, hills, holes or wrecks not too far out of the way, I should troll alongside them. Fish gather in and around underwater structures. Avoid dragging the lure directly over shallow reefs and sensitive corals.

As *Angel* motored along, I alternated between staring at the motionless fishing reel and at my fingernails, which I was sure were growing longer. I'd just lost the nail clippers over the side when using it to trim fishing line. That was not a lucky start to the day. When I ducked below to retrieve a snack, something grabbed the lure and briefly spun the reel. I eased *Angel's* throttle and cranked in a catch that wasn't putting up much of a fight.

"What is it?" Bill radioed, watching the action from the nearby *Defiant*. I had no idea. Wearing gloves, I raised the leader and gawked at the oddity dangling from the lure. The pop-eyed creature was five-inches long, not much larger than the lure. Its cavernous mouth, lined with needle like teeth, managed to fit over the hook. The fish's slimy body was pale.

"It's probably some kind of lizardfish," Bill said after I described it to him. "I wouldn't eat that." A pliers or de-hooking tool are handy for hook removal. I released the fish, which swam away with hasty vigor, and resumed trolling speed.

Later, when the sixth lizardfish attacked the lure, this one fatally injuring itself on the hook, I felt squeamish and put the rig away. It was apparent that these active creatures would just keep biting and needlessly harming their oversized mouths, no thanks to me.

Trolling across the Gulf Stream offers a chance to catch blue water species. For the best luck, troll along weed lines, current changes, and past floating debris. Fish, hoping to ferret out food, congregate around the flotsam found in weed lines. Diving seabirds is another sign of fish activity and the pros always head for the hovering frigate birds. Midday, something unidentifiable and serpentine squirmed off the lure when I reeled it in.

Later, I dropped the spoon along Florida's east coast while strictly sailing. The lure frequently caught floating weeds. Rubber skirts, when assembled correctly with the hook's tip just hidden by the skirt's fringe, are less apt to snag weeds.

When *Angel* sailed past an underwater ridge, the line whizzed off the reel. I eased the main and staysail, but left the Yankee pulling. *Angel* slowed to a crawl, the autopilot still keeping her on course. I cranked in some line and the fish, a barracuda, yanked it back out. This tug of war continued and I grew tired before my quarry did.

With the potential of ciguatera poisoning, large barracudas aren't on the menu. A "lip grip" tool, found in tackle shops, holds the wriggling fish so you can use long nosed pliers to safely remove the hook from its boney, razor edged jaw.

After only two and a half days of use in various locations, the trolling rig caught six lizardfish, a snake thing, three barracuda, and numerous nibbles from unseen fish lips. Still intent on catching something edible, I used a minnow shaped jig baited with bread while resting at anchor in Florida's shallow backwaters. A tiny pinfish was brought aboard and released. When a larger grunt hit the jig, I finally had a legal-sized keeper and a long awaited fish dinner.

A net is good for boating small fish, while a gaff is used for larger fish. A dash of cheap booze, delivered to the fish's mouth or gills with a turkey baster or squirt gun, usually works to quickly subdue a fish. This is less traumatic to the innocent living creature than trying to club the poor fellow on the head while it struggles, bleeds all over, and crashes around in the boat.

When a larger fish is caught while trolling, most cruisers find it easiest to gaff the fish, knock it out with booze, gut it and let it drag in the water behind the boat to minimize the mess. This is likely to attract sharks, so one must be diligent.

I scaled and cleaned my modest catch inside a bucket. Helpful gear includes gloves, long handled net or a gaff, de-hooker, needle nose pliers, a bucket, cheap booze and a method to deliver it, plastic cutting board and fillet knives. Fishing can add extra interest, and possibly fresh dinner, to a cruiser's travels.

* * *

42

Living Aboard a Small Boat:
Money, Basic Needs, and Comforts

For those unfamiliar with liveaboard boating, the lifestyle isn't unlike that of the RV traveler. We are comfortable living in smaller spaces with fewer amenities, so that we can more easily follow our nomadic interests and explore. For most liveaboard boat owners, being mobile means keeping things simple and not being weighed down by too many possessions. Houseboats, those beauties that enjoy a waterfront view and aren't built for long distance traveling, have greater domestic space and luxuries.

It's up to the individual's interests, and size of the vessel, how simple or luxurious one's living space will be. Some people enjoy camping in the wilds and don't mind foregoing a shower or two. Others prefer to make liberal use of a water maker inside an air conditioned cabin. The larger the vessel, the more amenities one can enjoy, though at an expense. There's no right or wrong answer and it doesn't matter what others think. The only thing that matters is what works for you and what's in the comfort zone of your wallet. For most of us, affordability is an issue.

Some people on shore seem to take offense at the live aboard cruiser's simpler comforts. They can be vociferously critical and discouraging toward people interested in pursuing the live aboard lifestyle. These types, typically isolated and taking things for granted, are ignorant of worldly things. They presume that we're avoiding taxes or are shirking social responsibility. Bill and I grumble about the numerous fees boaters pay. We're stuck with demands such as dock rent, marina fees, boat registration fees, sales taxes, fishing licenses, insurance, and income tax.

Those new to cruising need not be swayed by any disparagement or misunderstanding. Those judgmental souls who are quickest to condemn someone else's lifestyle are the ones most dissatisfied with their own mundane lives. Content, happy individuals are not into malicious criticism. Those are the types you'd rather associate with anyway.

$ Earning an Income $

Other misconceptions include the erroneous belief that only the privileged can sail away, live aboard, and island hop. That somehow, all of us traveling boaters are either recipients of a lottery, trust fund, or some secret cache of treasure. Those who were not in the know sometimes presumed that I was living off some inheritance or had wealthy parents. Though it would be nice if that were true, it isn't.

The majority of traveling cruisers rely on things like resourcefulness, skill building, and stubborn dedication. Most of us work and earn while underway. I've met numerous artists, photographers, musicians, magicians, and writers; their trades highly portable. One boater I met had a small machine shop in his trawler and earned an income with his machinist skills. Another was a welder. When not painting or writing, I repair marine engines and onboard electrical systems, which is another low overhead, portable trade.

Holding a captain's license for over 30 years now, Bill can be hired to operate vessels from large sportfishers to sailboats. Licensed captains also earn extra income doing boat deliveries. I've also met cruisers who work through the internet. One fellow created architectural drawings using a program on his laptop and communicated his designs to the main office via internet. Another was a computer programmer. I've also met a number of teachers. They'd work during the school season and cruise during the summer when school let out.

Traveling boaters tend to develop skills in numerous areas. If one trade is slow, another job can be done in the mean time. Seasonal or part time jobs ashore can be secured to help with marina slip fees, boat upkeep, and saving for the next cruise. Earning an income while living aboard and traveling is usually not as easy or as predictable as a steady, secure 9 to 5 job. These are trade offs that one typically contends with to cruise and live aboard.

Cost to Live Aboard

The costs to care for an active cruising vessel are also an important concern for those interested in living aboard. The amount one spends depends on the vessel's size and type. Power vessels will of course accrue significant fuel expenses. Sailboats need to occasionally invest in new sails, rigging and rope.

Costs also vary whether one stays at a marina (higher expense), a mooring field (moderate expense), or anchors out (minimal expense). Marinas charge by the foot, the vessel's length, and their rates vary depending on location. Mooring fields are more reasonably priced and the marinas operating them may or may not include basic amenities such as marina showers and laundry. Sometimes, shower and laundry room privileges are offered at extra cost. Anchoring out has its own share of hassles; one has to contend with rough weather traveling back and forth in a dinghy, and it's more difficult to bring in water and supplies.

Hauling out, outfitting an older vessel, or customizing a boat to one's own comforts can be a sizeable expense. Because I did most of my own work, I spent only about twelve thousand American dollars for *Angel's* extensive refit, a deal in the greater scheme of things. Over the next few years, I spent another ten thousand on additional customizations, charts, gear, more electronics, more solar panels, rope, and associated hardware.

Once a vessel and dinghy is outfitted and ready to travel, there are the lesser maintenance expenses: tools, spare parts, cosmetic upkeep, and repairs. Adding to the electrical system, such as including more solar panels or a wind generator is a chunk of change. Food, clothing, toiletries and personal items also need to be budgeted for. Boat insurance and health/dental insurance is also important to budget for if necessary. And don't forget related recreational items; fishing gear, diving equipment, tank refills, wetsuits or related apparel, and snorkel gear.

Overall, I'd surmise that my own monthly costs, including living expenses and boat costs, have been equivalent to or slightly more than what I was paying for with a monthly mortgage and utility bills as a homeowner; about one thousand a month. This cost is only an average though. Some months, little is spent. Other months, such as during haul outs or larger projects, a lot more is spent.

I also tend to be frugal, and for most boat repairs and chores, do the work myself instead of hiring someone. While cruising, expenditures mostly go toward food, dining out, dinghy gas and diesel, services like laundry and taxis, and the occasional repair. I prefer to anchor, so much is saved on marina fees. It's difficult not to be so vague about expenditures, but this lifestyle does not have a financial routine and it's difficult to pin exact numbers down. Each day is different.

Insurance

Most boat owners have marine insurance, though the rates can be expensive for older vessels. Other mariners would prefer to invest money into secure anchoring systems and top notch safety gear. Towing insurance is also available, where boat owners pay a reasonable annual fee for a useful service. It only costs me about $150 a year for unlimited towing, but *Angel* hasn't utilized it yet. Should she need it though, it's worth every penny.

Health and dental insurance varies depending on the individual. Combat veterans have insurance through the government. Others have employer sponsored medical insurance and most retirees are eligible for Medicare. The self employed usually pay a monthly premium for insurance, which can take a bite out of one's budget. I haven't yet found a reasonable, easy solution apart from the monthly premiums for the self employed, but recent health care reforms might be promising.

The Liveaboard Cabin: Inside and Out

Freshwater

Again, to use the RV comparison, a live aboard cruising vessel is wonderfully self contained, at least for a while. Eventually, the freshwater tanks will need refilling, unless a vessel is equipped with a watermaker, and fuel tanks need topping off, and the galley requires restocking.

Angel doesn't have a watermaker, but I did build a rain catching system using her bimini top. The rainwater is filtered before being introduced into the main tank. Water in her main tank also runs through an RV-style water filtration system. The water tank is kept fresh with colloidal silver instead of chemicals or bleach. Colloidal silver can be found in health food stores and a popular marine store used to sell it. For years now, I've been making my own with distilled water, amber glass containers, and pure, medical grade silver. (No, I haven't turned blue yet.)

To retrieve water while at anchor, cruisers use jerry jugs to transport water, which is obtained from the nearest marina or public dock. On *Angel*, I built a basic water retrieval system where a hose and 12-volt pump withdraws water from the jerry jug while it sits in the dinghy. It pumps the water into the main tank without the back-straining hassle of lugging the jugs.

Electricity

Deep cycle battery banks are used to provide power for the vessel's systems; lights, fans, pumps, and radios. Deep cycle batteries can also start the engine, but many boaters use separate starting batteries for this task. Battery bank size and capacity depends on how much power one needs and utilizes. Battery capacity should match demand, and batteries must be regularly recharged for long, reliable life. There are excellent how-to books for learning about a small boat's electrical system.

Batteries are charged by these most common methods; the engine's alternator, a battery charger plugged into shore power or portable AC generator, solar power, and wind. For example, *Angel's* deep cycle battery bank has a modest 420 amp hour capacity. Her charging system includes 305 watts of solar power and a DualPro marine battery charger powered by a generator. *Angel* does not have a separate starting battery for the diesel. Also, I avoid allowing my bank to be discharged below 12.2 volts before a recharging cycle.

This is easier said than done. *Defiant* enjoys the benefits of a wind generator along with solar panels for daily recharging.

Toilet

The toilet, known as the "head," is also RV-like in its compact, non standard size. Most marine toilets draw seawater in to flush, and waste is stored in a holding tank until it can be pumped out at a marina or by a pump out boat. Some vessels are equipped with treatment systems that sterilize the waste. Other boaters are using composting heads to avoid the hassles of contending with pump outs.

Local municipalities that desire to control mariners who anchor out often play the overused boaters-are-dumping-sewage card to sway public opinion against the live aboard. This can be a sensitive subject and bringing it up rouses just as much angry volatility as the topics of politics or religion.

In the past, some of the most widely read cruising icons had no heads at all and used a bucket. I'm not condoning this, but feel compelled to mention it. In these crowded modern times, most localities have posted regulations preventing the discharge of raw sewage.

Temperature Control

For boats cruising in the tropics, 12-volt powered cabin fans help keep things cool. Cabin top sun shades are also extremely helpful while at rest and when it's not too windy. On the water at anchor, one's surrounds tend to be breezier and cooler. Usually.

During those times when I am stuck in warmer latitudes, at anchor, and the breeze is defunct, I utilize a small, household air conditioner. It's a basic, single room unit. Powered by a portable generator, the air conditioning unit will quickly cool down *Angel's* cabin. Larger vessels can be, and often are, equipped with built in marine air conditioning. They also have internal generators to power the AC. Boats at the dock have the easier option of plugging into shore power.

In colder temperatures, boats will use small, camp style gas heaters or, if plugged into a dock, electric heaters. Care must be taken when using these.

Food Preparation

Galleys vary, depending on the vessel's size. Most small cruisers have two-burner stoves powered by propane or stove alcohol. Electric stoves require a significant power demand. Larger boats are also are equipped with small ovens.

Refrigeration is often a concern for smaller vessels. *Angel* uses a quality portable unit specifically for marine use. It resembles a mid-sized cooler and is powered by 12-volts. The key is to assure that there's enough battery capacity to keep the refrigerator running. Other small cruising boats use insulated iceboxes, which are basically built in coolers. Usually block ice is used and the melt water is routed into the bilge. Boaters with these are always questing for ice at every port.

Cruising With Pets

Nonhuman crewmembers typically need to have special paperwork, such as certificates of health from the veterinarian, and usually an import permit, when checking in to other ports. Each country varies and you must research ahead of time what their specific requirements are. For example, the Bahamas requires an import permit for each pet (about $10. each) and a health certificate from the pet's veterinarian in the States. These papers are then shown to the customs officer upon check in.

House Keeping

I'm unable to help having a prissy side and an insistence on keeping a clean cabin with decent living comforts. This particular drive has caused me to find less typical solutions. For example, on a website devoted to selling goods to truckers, I've found boat friendly 12-volt powered items. The 12-volt mini vacuum cleaners and DC to DC converter were especially useful.

There are also coffee makers, but they draw a significant amount of amperage. One ingenious boater showed me how to make coffee by converting a ground filled coffee filter into a teabag. The filter and its contents are tightly secured with a clean clothes pin. The "teabag" filter is submerged in boiling water and briefly steeped. It's the same thing a coffee maker does.

Nontoxic cleaning solutions such as ordinary white vinegar in a spray bottle help keep the cabin interior surfaces clean. The vinegar kills mildew. Should a boat have a flush-type marine head, vinegar's also the best for cleaning the head's internals without harming the rubber valve and o-rings. It also helps keep sanitation hoses clear and free from crystallized deposits.

In warm latitudes, flying cockroaches sometimes wing into one's vessel, and non-flying ones travel aboard hidden in bags. Boric acid tablets, found in the pest control section in general stores, have worked for me. Boric acid, made from a mineral called boron, kills bugs after it is ingested. Bill also found success with the usual roach baits. Avoid placing these items within reach of children or pets.

Hygiene

Small cruising boat showering facilities might be anything from the camping solar heated bags to steamy, pressure water showers heated by the engine. I've even seen people bathing in saltwater (it felt unpleasantly sticky after trying that), to jumping out in the rain (I wimped out when it felt too cold). Staying at a marina allows a boater to utilize land based facilities.

What's frustrating to many smaller sailboat owners is the lack of an actual, indoor shower stall. I had to get creative, but simple, when building *Angel's* shower system. I installed a plastic shower curtain that folds away after it's dry. A shallow, wide plastic tub serves as the shower stall's water collecting system. I pour the collected shower water down the sink when done. It's awkward, but worth the hassle, as I'd rather avoid rotting parts of *Angel's* cabin floor woodwork by allowing the shower water to drain into the bilge. Shower water in the bilge also becomes odiferous.

Many boats have separate tanks and sumps for this very thing. *Angel's* shower water is heated by a rectangular solar tank on her cabin roof. In cloudy weather, I heat water on the stove and pour it into one of two shower tanks, which are separate from the main water tank. Shower water is drawn out with a 12-volt pressure pump. A second shower system is in the cockpit. Many boats like having freshwater cockpit showers for rinsing dive gear and generally cooling off in hot weather while cruising.

Washing Clothes

Laundry is typically done at a marina, which provides these services, or, if anchored out, at a Laundromat. If away from shore for long periods, cruisers will hand wash a few select articles of clothing, depending on water availability. Larger vessels sometimes are equipped with their own miniature washer and drier.

On larger island settlements, Laundromats can be found and are usually within walking distance. Laundry bags can be transported using a folding, wheeled dolly. Cruisers love using these for everything including groceries, laundry, booze runs, and jerry jugs.

Entertainment

For entertainment, boaters install 12-volt marine or automotive stereo systems onboard. Laptop computers can be powered by the boat's own DC battery source with power supply cords usually known as 'car charging cords' or 'DC to DC power cords.' Computers utilize DC power anyways, and many laptops use about 19 volts.

Many cruisers watch movies on the laptop's DVD player, or from a digital data storage device. A small set of external speakers, available at most electronic stores, offers better sound for movie watching on a laptop. Since *Defiant* and *Angel* have stereo systems with speakers, a jack can be plugged in to the stereo and the laptop for a dramatic, surround sound effect.

Some boats have large, flat screen TVs. These can be connected to satellite television broadcasting systems such as Direct TV. I know cruisers who enjoy these and the TV receiver is a small satellite dish that rotates to maintain the signal and works even at anchor.

Marinas frequently provide book exchanges and cruisers often enjoy trading books when meeting others in remote areas.

Bringing the Kids

I've been seeing more and more young families with kids enjoying the boating life. Many will travel for a few years before settling down with their growing families. From what I've seen, kids who have been exposed to the real world experience of travel and cruising greatly benefit from it. They learn new things, enjoy a variety of educational opportunities, and expand their base of knowledge. This life experience gives them a valuable, well rounded perspective that's carried into their adult lives.

With no children of my own, I don't have inside knowledge on what it's like to raise kids on boats, but I know what it's like to grow up as one of those kids. It adds interest and a change of pace from video games or being anesthetized by television. I am immensely grateful to my parents for enriching my life in this way.

The Dinghy

Especially for anchored out mariners, the dinghy is a valuable asset to the cruising life. The dinghy needs to be sturdy enough to safely transport people and gear, and handle weather, and yet be light enough to transport. This is a conundrum all small cruising boat owners face and probably haven't yet found the perfect answer for.

A cruising friend who loved the easy storage of a plastic, folding dinghy wasn't so thrilled by its lightweight flimsiness during an unexpected squall. The dinghy, engine and all, flipped in a sudden build up of waves. He was unhurt, but had lost important personal items and an expensive outboard.

On the other end of the dinghy spectrum, many people appreciate the stability of a rigid bottom inflatable (RIB) and its ability to handle fast outboards. Smaller cruisers have difficulties safely transporting a RIB during open water crossings. They are heavy and troublesome to deflate and arrange on deck. Boaters towing the dinghy risk loosing it should there be a surprise storm. Inflatables also have that pesky habit of not remaining inflated.

Our friends from *Escape* had an inflatable with a semi-rigid floor, I believe, that rolled up for storage. They could completely deflate and store the dinghy on board in a small space. This was extremely convenient. The trade off was the boat couldn't take a larger outboard, so it took longer to putt to and from land. Adverse current or rough waters also made things uncomfortable. There was also the splash factor.

Babette was always joking about how her skirt would end up board stiff from the salt water spray.

Defiant used to have a RIB, but now carries a small fiberglass dinghy in his davits. The dinghy is cat-hulled, giving it an extra measure of stability for its small size. Plastic hard dinghies seem to be increasing in popularity, but I have no experience using them. Fellow boaters who own them appreciate the plastic dinghy's light weight, but report that they feel be "tippy" and unstable. Importantly, what ever the dinghy is and if it's equipped with an outboard, it's also a good idea to carry oars or a paddle onboard. A small anchor is also recommended.

The above is only a basic foundation regarding living aboard and cruising. There is no right or wrong and an individual's choices are based on their own unique interests, needs, budget, and how long or far they want to travel. Each boat, power, sail, or houseboat, is unique and will have unique requirements. Each person is different and will have specific preferences. That is what makes cruising and meeting others so interesting.

* * *

Photo by fellow cruiser Curtis Craig

About the author:
Rebecca Burg works as a marine mechanic and solo sails her Bayfield cutter, *Angel*. Captain Bill Robinson is a fishing guide and solo sails his 36' ketch, *Defiant*. They're completing a second decade of maritime adventures.

www.rebeccaburg.com
www.keywest-sportfish.com

Acknowledgments

A special thank you to friends and family for their help
and invaluable influence in the creation of this book.
The author is solely responsible for any grammatical errors.

Captain Bill Robinson. The main character in this book.

Claire Perrault. A hard-to-describe, remarkable woman with keen intellect and many talents. She's currently sharing her weaving and artistic talents with the Key West community.

Curtis Craig. Cruiser and owner of a parrot-ruled Westsail. Some of his work involves keeping large ships attached to the dock.

Neil Braun. Sailboat owner, co-owner of R. Burg's Small Engine Service, and driver of *Workboat Car-54*

Steve Morrell. Sailor and magazine editor who encouraged me to write for the public in the first place.

Enthusiastic readers and fellow adventurers like Crazy Kenny, Scuba Tony, Lyle, Caveman Fred, Captain Randy, and many more, all who've shared their stories while enriching my own life experience. *Everyone* has a story worth sharing....